E. Hughes

ENABLING LEADERSHIP

Second edition

To Elizabeth and James Jaap
The first enablers I had the good fortune to encounter

Enabling Leadership

Achieving results with people

Second edition

Tom Jaap

Gower

First published 1986 by HRA Publications

Second edition published by
Gower Publishing Company Limited,
Gower House,
Croft Road,
Aldershot
Hants GU11 3HR,
England

Gower Publishing Company
Old Post Road
Brookfield
Vermont 05036
USA

British Library Cataloguing in Publication Data

Jaap, Tom
  Enabling leadership.—2nd ed.
  1. Personnel management – Manuals
  I. Title
  658.3

Library of Congress Cataloging-in-Publication Data

Jaap, Tom, 1936–
  Enabling leadership.
  1. Leadership. I. Title.
HM141.J17 1989   303.3'4   88–24719

ISBN 0 566 02783 6

Printed and bound in Great Britain at
The Camelot Press Ltd, Southampton

Contents

Preface

This book is designed to allow you to build an understanding of enabling leadership using a holistic approach.

Part I sets the scene by providing a vision of the year 2000 and beyond which I believe can be achieved using an enabling process. This part provides you with a wide-angled view of the future and of the concept and practice of enabling leadership. It provides a sound base on which you can explore in detail each of the components in Parts II and III.

Part II explains the foundation components and gives the reader an insight into what makes an enabling leader: enabling awareness, philosophy and learning are the three pillars on which enabling leadership can be developed. These insights are needed to understand the enabling process in Part III.

Part III lets you explore the application of enabling leadership in developing an enabling organization where the environment created encourages individuals to make an effective contribution.

I start conceptually with the whole, examine the parts, and then re-examine the whole in action. The intention is to provide you with ample scope to adapt, interpret and add your own dimension to enabling leadership. I have not attempted to provide all the answers as I believe each of us needs to translate enabling leadership into our own language and develop our own enabling philosophy and practice.

Some concepts appear more than once and are included to reinforce their significance to the enabling process.

Enabling leadership needs to be experienced to feel its power.

This has been the general comment and feedback from people who have known about the concept and practice but have not been able fully to understand and internalize it – until, that is, they have participated in an enabling leadership workshop.

Acknowledgements

The process of writing about enabling leadership has involved a host of people who have contributed in many ways to its development. Their help has come in many different forms and in a variety of situations over the years. The people are too numerous to detail here. However, their contribution is appreciated and acknowledged. Many of the contributors are participants on our learning events and from their sharing and exchanging we been able to refine and develop the enabling concept and practice.

Two people in particular have played a significant part in the production of the book. I should like to acknowledge Mary Brooks for reading and commenting on the text and Sheila Hampshire who pulled the resources together to enable the book to emerge.

Part I
SETTING THE SCENE

Suggests how a positive society can be achieved with enabling leadership

Chapter 1 WHY ENABLING LEADERSHIP?
CONTRIBUTION CULTURE

Chapter 2 BEYOND THE YEAR 2000
POTENTIAL BRAKES ON THE FUTURE
CREATING THE FUTURE
UNDERSTANDING THE PARADOXES
STRATEGIC DIRECTIONS
SCENARIO FOR THE YEAR 2000 AND BEYOND
ENABLING LEADERSHIP

Chapter 3 OVERVIEW OF ENABLING LEADERSHIP
THE EMERGING ENABLER
ENABLING AWARENESS
ENABLING PHILOSOPHY
ENABLING LEARNING
ENABLING OUTPUTS
ENABLING ROLES
ENABLING PROCESS
–(1) Enabling Organization
–(2) Enabling Contribution
ENABLING CHANGE
SUMMARY

1 Why enabling leadership?

People today are seeking new kinds of relationships with each other and with the organizations with which they associate. They want to work in a more collaborative way which allows them to make a valued contribution. Observing how an increasing number of organizations are changing, I am confident that a contribution process will emerge as an effective vehicle to tap the energy, skill and commitment of people. The contribution process requires a culture which actively includes people in the decision-making process, particularly when the decisions affect their lives. It also requires considerable change in the behaviour of those who 'manage' others as it challenges the traditional nature of managing with its dogmatic concern with control and discipline. In organizations today the contribution process is achieving results 'with' people rather than 'through' people.

The collaborative language of contribution indicates how it represents a vastly different organization culture, in which people expect to work in an open and trusting style with each other. All will have the opportunity to be involved in shaping the organization by making their contribution to arrive at a shared vision of the future. This process enables all members to 'buy into' the organization and be committed to assisting it achieve its goals, which will be shared goals. Consistency will be the watchword as interpersonal transactions are based on a genuine desire to understand each other.

3

CONTRIBUTION CULTURE

A principal attribute of a contribution culture is its goal orientation. When those involved in the organization are aware of the aims, they understand what their contribution should be and how it can be made. They readily accept that it is only the committed effort of all which produces the desired goals; and that if necessary they should give more to assist others achieve, as in the end it will benefit them all.

Depending on your personal experience and mind set you will acknowledge that the behaviour required by people operating within a contribution culture is significantly different from that which exists in many organizations today. The challenge is how to make the transition to transform the organization effectively. Enabling leadership is a process which provides people with a clear set of guidelines on how to make the transition whilst retaining the best of what already exists in their organizations.

The answer lies in the ability to confront issues and effect change in an enabling manner. To achieve this there are many challenges we need to confront and resolve. If you can conquer the three listed below, it will make a significant difference in the future:

- Coping with change
- Traditional thinking
- Leadership.

Coping with change

We live in one of the most rapidly changing periods in the development of global society. The speed of change, being brought about by a bewildering complexity of factors, requires people to develop different skills and attitudes. The uncertainty created by rapid change affects people to different degrees; some are excited by the opportunities and challenges which change brings whilst others fear the resulting problems and uncertainty.

We focus first on people who perceive change as a threat. Many are adversely affected by change and do not know how to cope. Typical reactions to change can be feelings of fear, anger, a sense of hopelessness and distress which triggers behaviour designed to fight (or flee from) the change and thus maintain the status quo. Another frequent response from those who find it difficult to cope is to expect others to act on their behalf as the cause of change is perceived to be outside their field of influence. Many call on government to provide solutions; however, as experience in many democratic countries shows, politicians tend to have relatively short-term goals. These dictate policies which result in palliative proposals designed to provide short-term rather than long-term solutions.

This response may be influenced by a prevailing view held by some governments that current problems are of a relatively short-term nature. However, as time passes this is recognized as a dangerous and very short-sighted attitude which must alter. People are coming to realize that the fundamental changes taking place in society require long-term solutions. I believe that we need leaders with a vision of the future who can create environments which gain the commitment of those involved to see it shaped for the benefit of all. These leaders will define appropriate strategic directions involving people in a process which enables change to be achieved in a positive manner.

This challenge requires determination from the new breed of enabling leaders so that they are not deflected from their urgent mission by traditionalists. A great deal of positive change has been actively resisted over the years by people who have a genuine desire to keep things just as they are. There have also been negative results of some changes in which little regard was taken of the good which existed in the situation – the baby was thrown out with the bathwater. All this tends to add weight to the arguments of those who resist change and makes them less interested in even exploring the potential for positive consequences emerging from change.

Enabling leaders create an environment which encourages those who see change as a challenge and who want to achieve the best results possible. They are inspired to take action which results in positive outcomes. Through their positive approach they influence others, who may be less determined or certain about what to do, to become involved in the process and work towards achieving effective results.

Traditional thinking

In many societies traditional thinking still encourages organizations to continue to base learning and development on a belief
in 'the sabre-toothed tiger curriculum syndrome'. This syndrome
emphasizes learning about, and acquiring skills from, the past.
However much we may value the past there is now an urgent
need to think about today and the future. Traditional thinkers
also draw heavily on reason and rational thinking to explain what
has happened and to extrapolate what may happen in the future.
In the past when inflation and interest rates were low and currency
fluctuations were almost unheard of it was relatively safe to use
reason to determine what a future state could be like. But in
today's climate of turbulent change we need to balance rational
and analytical thinking with creative and lateral thinking. What
works today provides no guarantee that it will work tomorrow.

We need to explore what the future may hold if we want to
identify the knowledge, skills and attitudes required which will
allow us to be effective. There is significant international support
for the view that new directions in learning and development are
long overdue. We should see a continuing move away from the
attitude of 'Let's fight to keep it as it is' to one of seeking solutions
which benefit all.

As we shall see in Chapter 5 we need to look 'outside the dots'
to find solutions which match the complex problems which exist.
The new leaders will have the capacity to handle a wide range of
situations using a problem-solving and solution-seeking process
which combines analytical with creative thinking.

Leadership

I am involved in a wide range of private and public organizations
in many countries around the world. This has allowed me to
observe how managers tackle decisions which range from learning
to cope with rapidly changing markets to understanding the
complex expectations of their people. The way they have
approached the solution of these, and other, problems has
provided me with a clear picture of how few of them actually
perform the role of being an effective leader. Even so, it is encour-

aging to see that managers are developing a growing awareness of how many of the current practices in organizations inhibit the use of people's existing abilities and latent talent.

Although there are many excellent books and programmes concerned with leadership, they tend to see leadership in terms of the traditional model of leader/follower: I believe that we are moving towards an era in which the philosophy and practice of self – and shared leadership will prevail.

By understanding the benefits of sharing our learning developments in an open way we can learn to collaborate to achieve significant advances in how leaders develop. We have developed a leadership model (Figure 1.1) which demonstrates how a leader's style changes with changes in the situation and organization.

The model is based on research into leadership in organizations over the past ten years. The attitudes and subsequent behaviour displayed by managers and the outcomes from the people managed were observed. The process clearly established that managers used a range of leadership styles in a variety of situations. We were able to differentiate when a style was used with positive results from those which produced negative results.

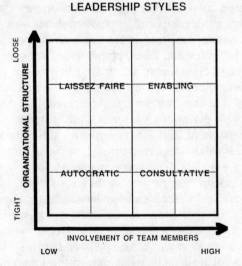

Figure 1.1 Leadership style model

Although there were many factors involved, we were able to identify two significant components which existed when managers acted as leaders and which could significantly affect the outcome.

A manager's philosophy

The first component relates to the philosophy of the managers and describes the way they involve others to create and sustain the social networks within the organization. Philosophy is recognized by the degree to which the values of mutual trust, respect for self and others, empathy, flexibility, concern for individual and team needs, participative decision making and interactive multi-path communications exist and are shared within the organization.

An organization's architecture

'Architecture' is the term we have given to the second component and it refers to the structure and procedures developed by the organization to enable its systems to operate. This is represented by the degree to which the organization operates an open or closed system to develop and apply its policies and procedures. In an open system the strategic plans, corporate policy, goals and objectives, job roles and tasks, planning and monitoring outputs and rewarding achievement are arrived at using a participative process. The outcome of this open process is a high level of commitment and contribution by all involved.

A manager's personal philosophy and attitudes will strongly influence the style of leadership even in an authoritarian organization, and this will be displayed through the action and behaviours used on the job. We need more managers to be aware of the style of leadership they project as they go about the business of managing others. Awareness and understanding will communicate to managers whether they are acting in a way which creates a positive or negative environment in their part of the organization. In a negative environment a manager tends to be locked into a limited range of leadership styles due to the inherent rigidity in the systems, his/her thinking and the people he/she works with.

In a positive environment a leader will be more flexible and use a wide range of leadership styles geared to the needs of the people involved and the circumstances surrounding the situation.

SITUATIONAL VS PREDICTABLE

This is where the enabling process can play an increasing and important part. Given any type of situation an enabling leader will use a leadership style which is congruent with the culture and designed to achieve a positive outcome from the process. The leader acknowledges any potentially dysfunctional factors in the environment and actively works to minimize their effect on people and their outputs. Therefore, enabling leaders work at creating environments which release the positive energy of all those involved to achieve effective results in all types of situations. Their organizations are characterized by a high degree of interpersonal and organizational flexibility which enables people to work in a synergistic way.

The book sets out to describe how to identify an enabler by what s/he does and how s/he goes about achieving effectiveness in all that s/he does. It aims to provide the reader with a clear picture of what it requires to be an enabling leader and some encouragement to develop further their enabling skills. Organizations and society urgently need more people who are prepared to be enabling leaders and who are willing to accept the challenge of shaping society and organizations into a more positive development mode and thus discover a greater number of win/win solutions.

I believe that we have many visionaries who continue to describe the future for us to take note. We also have many people doing a fine job as enablers helping to translate the visions into reality. Together they will enable change to be carried out in a way which empowers people. The process will be based on empowering others by helping them all to be self-sufficient within a philosophy of caring for others.

It is against this backcloth that I see enabling leadership emerge as an effective way to meet the challenge of the future. Enabling leadership is based on a philosophy and practice which can assist people to adapt positively to changing circumstances. For example, as we are in an age of high technology, it is essential for us to make increasing use of these capabilities. This can enable us to make better use of our brain power by applying our thinking to produce creative solutions to many of societies problems and opportunities.

2 Beyond the year 2000

In recent years I have developed a growing interest in the future. Involvement with a number of national training and development organizations around the world provides opportunities to express my ideas on what I see might be the major challenges. I have received many invitations to present my paper 'Strategic Directions in Human Resource Development' (HRD). And as the picture took on a greater global shape, I modified the paper to reflect the expanding dimensions and added the word 'International' before HRD to reflect this shift of emphasis. Visiting at least six countries a year enables me to assess further the issues particular to each country and allows me to continue to build a sharper picture.

Therefore looking into the future for me is a major activity stimulated by the positive feedback I received. Encouraged by this response, I continue to seek ways of improving my understanding of the factors which appear to influence the future. It is exciting to learn how to identify the factors, which I call 'indicators', to attempt to understand the impact they could have on people in the future. This process naturally led me to become much more strategic in my thinking and open to the various possible scenarios which appeared. In developing my strategic thinking I built the following model which helped me to make sense of the process and obtain increasing clarity (Figure 2.1).

Figure 2.1 represents the way I have learned to look at the changing world. I use it to construct and put shape to the environment by following five basic steps:

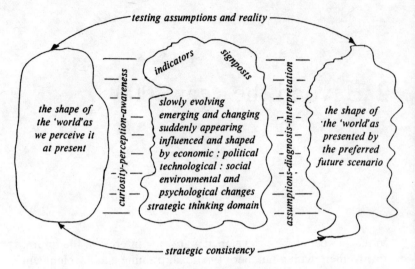

Figure 2.1 **Stategic thinking model**

- scan the environment to spot indicators
- assess the significance of each indicator on its own and clustered with others to see if trends emerge
- analyze the trends to determine what could be the main strategic signposts indicating future strategic HRD directions
- use the signposts to compose a number of future scenarios
- select from these scenarios the strategic directions which can be used to construct a preferred future scenario.

The model provides me with a flexible process which enables different, yet relevant, maps of reality to be developed and tested. The maps which have emerged excite me and, I believe, will excite others. This book is the vehicle I have chosen to communicate how I see the future and how I believe it can be realized through enabling leadership.

The key to shaping the future in a way which is beneficial for all lies in the vision we have, coupled with a commitment to strive and see it realized. I have every confidence in the fact that we have the people with the vision and skills to construct a future which offers hope and fulfilment. We shall be given the opportunity to plan the transition to a transformed society which has resolved most of the problems which beset us today. Having a vision which is based on a number of shared human values will provide us with a framework to confront the apathy and helplessness many people around the world feel. I believe that we are much closer than is realized to releasing the energy in people to act constructively.

POTENTIAL BRAKES ON THE FUTURE

As I constructed a number of strategic maps and discussed their implications with friends and colleagues two main factors kept emerging which were perceived to be the main brakes on society ever realizing the vision I had of the future. Therefore, before I unfold my vision of a preferred future scenario I shall explore two potential brakes on change:

- the historical perspective
- the focus on deviants.

Historical perspective

Being involved in the international people developmental business gives me ample opportunities to meet a large number of people. The more I become involved in strategic thinking the more I am aware of how many people appear to live in the past. Time and again I observe discussions on change being blocked by individuals whose case rests on what has happened in the past. They are generally unwilling to accept that the criteria surrounding today's situations could be different.

On closer examination, several factors kept surfacing which encourage individuals to stay linked to the past:

- their attention is very much on day-to-day details which encourages them to develop a fixation on current matters
- when confronted with decisions about the future they tend to state difficulties or seek solutions from past experiences which results in a slow and often inappropriate reponse as the circumstances have changed in the meantime
- they tend to perceive their organizations and jobs in historical

and static terms; they are generally unwilling to consider changes in structure or different working patterns
- lack of perception in terms of seeing that anything needs to be done coupled with a confused reaction and almost contrived 'blindness' to the effects of rapid technological and social change.

Stability vs ambiguity

In order to explore the causes of the malady and why the response to change has been slow and largely negative, look at Western Europe in general and business in particular.

Much has happened, particularly over the last decade, to change the way many people work. Technology has significantly changed the daily routine of masses of people. At the same time, response to adverse economic realities has resulted in a substantial drive for higher productivity coupled with reduction in numbers employed. These two factors together have created a great deal of change and uncertainty which continue to leave many confused and apprehensive of what the future may hold. Our response to this challenge has been patchy and may be partly attributed to:

- lack of ability to perceive the rate of change
- speed of change itself which does not provide, as previously, the same time to understand what is happening
- our slow and generally negative reaction to change
- lack of leadership which enables individuals to learn how to adapt effectively to change
- fear of change
- attitudes and expectations more in tune with times of greater relative stability.

Raised expectations

In addition, expectations were raised during the years of rapid growth. From the early 1970s large numbers of people experienced the material and other pleasures which used to be the preserve of the wealthy. It is also generally accepted now that people are better educated and informed which gives them greater choice about what they can do with their lives. This has resulted in individuals becoming more independent and wanting a greater say in shaping the environment in which they live.

However, individuals face a paradox in that the more involvement they desire, the stronger is the authorities' determination to preserve the status quo. People are constantly faced with situations in which their freedom is restricted. This usually involves limits to the degree of freedom and choice in all aspects of their lives. Industry and commerce are only now beginning to realize that the world has changed. No longer is it considered acceptable for people to be used as units of production to be manipulated by remote bosses.

As the impetus for human rights gains momentum and support through the legislative process, individuals increasingly question the need for many of the following business practices:

- clocking on and off work
- working regular hours per day, days per week
- doing jobs in unsuitable conditions
- being seen as cogs in a wheel and not consulted on matters which directly affect them, as that is the prerogative of management
- being controlled and disciplined in ways which demotivate and make them feel inadequate
- traditional leadership linked to hierarchical and authoritarian organizations which treat people as subordinates and followers.

The result is tension and conflict as each side perceives its rights and acts to force the other to conform. It is a tragedy to see so much energy being invested in maintaining the status quo. We need to refocus our energies on learning from the past so that we don't make the same mistakes again. As change is accelerated by new developments we need to understand that yesterday's successes cannot be guaranteed to be tomorrow's successes.

The comfort and security enjoyed in the past are unlikely ever to return. The one certainty at the present time is our need to be able to cope with change. This will challenge us to break from the chains of the past and discard historical baggage so that we can approach the future with an open and expectant mind. Just as certainty provided comfort we can learn to feel good about, and able to face and cope with, uncertainty. We can learn to handle change by shaping the future with our ability to think to the future.

By developing a more open and enlightened perspective we can learn to identify where to channel our energies and talents to effect change and improve our organizations in particular, and society as a whole. We shall build on the sound experiences of the past which have given us positive benefits. In addition, as we learn to be more creative, we shall construct new experiences which will help us make a significant leap forward. By learning to look at situations from different perspectives, we shall be able to perceive where the blockages are and what we should do to remove them.

The deviant minority

Observing how different managements respond to internal and external issues which confronted their organizations made me acutely aware of the negative bias of their responses. Exploring further, I saw that many of their decisions are made in reaction to some relatively minor act or incident. When focusing particularly on incidents involving people, it was revealing to see how many decisions were made in reaction to minor deviant behaviour. On closer examination I found that the individuals provoking this reaction represented a very small percentage of the total numbers involved. Yet it was in response to the behaviour of this negative and deviant minority that management made decisions such as:

- changes in supervision to discourage individuals from behaving in the unacceptable manner so as to ensure the situation did not recur
- restrictions imposed as new or stricter rules, regulations, procedures and systems designed to tighten control and strengthen discipline
- offenders being punished through misuse of the normal disciplinary procedure
- punitive action designed to teach a lesson to anyone in the organization who might be tempted to misbehave in a similar fashion.

It is startling to stand back and examine the outcomes of such decisions.The adverse effects on the majority involved in the organization arising out of the action of the deviant minority are significant. Many of the decisions produced further perceived restrictions on the freedom of individuals who were unlikely to be involved in any deviant behaviour.

The majority tend not to react vociferously as they have learned to expect such reaction. Managements observe the apparent silence/acceptance and conclude that they have acted effectively. However, the covert reaction tends to be adverse and generally result in negative attitudes being reinforced and with continued demotivation. Management eventually becomes aware of demotivation through declining performance and productivity. And, what might be the expected reaction by managment to improve performance . . . ? Why, tougher action designed to enforce systems and procedures to gain greater control over the situation. The end result? Each side is trapped in a self-fulfilling prophecy which reinforces the 'them and us' syndrome.

Meanwhile the deviants, having served their sentences, continue their lives largely unaffected by the effect on others of their actions and in most instances with their behaviour unchanged.

It is sad to reflect that we can still experience this process in organizations today. It seems that some managements have still to learn to understand the destructive power of the deviant minority.

Focus on the positive majority

One of the most important challenges we face today is reversing the focus on the deviant minority and redirecting our attention onto the positive majority. The benefits to be derived are substantial and will better fit the needs and aspirations of the rising generation. Individuls are becoming more assertive about their rights, and will be less inclined passively to accept the situations described above. In addition, the negative focus tends to blind us to the substantial proportion of positive work and significant contributions being made by individuals.

Our task is to direct attention onto those who are making a positive contribution. We need to remove the 'blinkers' and learn how to replace the demotivating effects of the negative focus by reshaping organizations and changing attitudes about people. My vision of the future will be realized through the efforts of individuals who are enablers. Many exist today and my mission is to encourage the development of environments which produce a climate within which they grow. To facilitate the process we need to break out of the bondage of the past and project ourselves into the future. The following sections provide ideas on how to 'let go' and start creating the future.

CREATING THE FUTURE

Investing in the future

There are many things which encourage me to invest time and effort in attempting to understand the future. Learning to 'let go' of the historical perspective provides many opportunities to explore the future from fresh perspectives. The natural tendency to evaluate everything said or done by an individual *vis-à-vis* our own experience is replaced by a willingness to listen and understand information from the individual's point of view. As I explore the future, awareness about myself increases. I begin to understand better the effect I have on others as we share ideas and visions. We recognize that the speed of change means that what happened yesterday may be of little value in predicting what might happen tomorrow. Understanding that change is a natural phenomenon helps to put the process into perspective as we witness its effects on us. Usually we can observe how we and others change with the years. For some, years appear to take a heavy toll; whilst others appear to enjoy every benefit change offers. In most instances, the outcome is largely dependent on the attitude adopted by the individual.

Looking forward can help develop an attitude of anticipation and excitement about opportunities the future offers. Change brings with it many problems and opportunities and the skill lies in being able to translate the problems into opportunities. Learning to look forward can provide the motivation to shape new perspectives to life and kindle the desire to take risk, Another skill is in being able to identify what you need to do to position yourself to gain the best advantage from your personal investment.

Identifying indicators can provide useful insights into what the future may hold.

Identifying indicators

I use the term 'indicator' to describe an issue, event or item of data which indicates a trend in one or more of the following main arenas: political, social, economic, technological and environmental. I have learned to look for indicators in every aspect of life without initially making a judgement on their significance. The fun is in capturing them, putting them into their appropriate category and then trying to interpret what they might tell you about the future.

The list which follows illustrates many of the trends to be found around the world. They are not placed in any order of significance:

Social

- career upheavals due to different requirements and fewer opportunities
- people living longer
- increasing interest in pursuits which enhance the quality of life
- individuals demanding a greater say in matters which could affect their lives at work, home, school and socially
- less time spent in 'work' with more time being allocated to 'non work' activities
- changing value systems with less regard for traditional authority and discipline
- decreasing/increasing birth rate
- increasing divide between the haves and have-nots
- relationships being shaped in different ways to meet many new needs
- substantial work needed to improve the infrastructure, care for the sick and needy and improve the living environment
- concern to feed the hungry and help them to be self-sufficient

Economic

- increasing numbers of people seeking employment
- fewer job opportunities
- output increasing through improved productivity and effective use of technology
- different roles, with greater accountability expected
- significant changes in world markets
- growing impact of newly industrializing countries on world markets
- increasing problem of Third World debt

Political

- increasing disenchantment with adversarial posturing as seen in business and politics
- people seeking more autonomy, information and involvement
- demands from minority groups for their own identity through development of culture, religion, education and community activities
- desire for longer timescale in decision making based on a consensus view of what would be best for all, rather than for sectional interests

Technological

- rapid development and widespread application of information technology
- deployment of communication satellites providing multi-communication channels
- biotechnology developments which offer potentially revolutionary outcomes
- robotics being used to achieve quality products with minimum labour inputs
- concern about adverse affects of technology on the environment, food and health

Environmental

- concern for protecting the environment and preserving finite resources
- pressure for nuclear disarmament
- more caring response to floods, droughts and other natural disasters
- desire for lifestyles which add value to the environment.

UNDERSTANDING THE PARADOXES

Although the indicators have been placed within the context of a particular arena, this does not accurately represent their inter-linking nature. The art is to assess which of the indicators will be significant signposts to the future. The fascinating array of indicators shows how much of the world offers many paradoxes. Declining industries in some countries can be found thriving in others. As drought is experienced in large areas of one continent, floods are being experienced elsewhere. Ageing populations can be found in many of the developed countries whereas in newly industrializing countries, and even more in undeveloped ones, the majority of the population is under 15.

As we all are part of the 'global village' it makes sense to broaden our perspective to see what industries exist in other countries and the influence they appear to be having on shaping the future there.

Having identified the indicators, the next stage is to select those which signal significant congruent trends. These now form what we call 'strategic signposts' which point to the future. We have selected the following signposts to illustrate this stage of the process. These strategic signposts relate specifically to people who:

- want more autonomy in deciding their future
- have a desire for collaborative arrangements
- want healthy life styles and preventive health care
- want to develop positive relationships
- see benefits from whole person development
- want different lifestyles and work patterns
- consider work and leisure as an integrated process

- are concerned to protect their environments
- want to make a contribution to local organizations
- have a desire to share with and care for others
- want to be respected and respect others
- see the value of working in small groups with which they can identify.

Some other signposts signal trends which relate more specifically to organizations, including:

- a move to decentralized organizations
- leadership styles designed to empower others
- information technology reshaping how we think
- fundamental changes in education and training as society responds to learning needs and styles
- assistance to 'those in need' based on what they want to achieve in their own terms and culture
- action taken to preserve our natural and finite resources
- technology bringing the 'global village' concept closer to reality and thus making countries more interdependent
- increasing demands for regional and local variations to meet the unique needs of different communities
- wide variations in how people relate in families.

The process involves a kaleidoscope of scenarios from the signposts and indicators, constructing every possible and many impossible scenarios. It is useful to take single signposts and indicators as a basis for projecting a future construct, followed by the formation of clusters to observe the outcome of their interaction. The most important ingredient at this stage is to suspend judgement and allow the creative part of our brain to take over.

STRATEGIC DIRECTIONS

Subsequent data processing provides a good opportunity to see if the signposts combine to make significant strategic directions. It is very important to uncover assumptions underpinning the strategic directions identified. Visualizing, identifying trends and testing assumptions is an ideal small-group activity which can be used to develop creative thinking and team work. Being able to bounce ideas off other people can stretch thinking and realize a wide range of new and constructive possibilities.

This stage in the process provides valuable insights on what may be strategic directions to the future and thus leads to positioning the main parts of the architecture on which to construct a preferred future scenario.

By using visioning and trend perception techniques, I identified a number of strategic directions (mini-scenarios), including the following:

- there would be ample work for all who wanted it
- people would try to relate to each other in empathetic ways designed to enable positive relationships to develop
- people would have a much greater say in shaping their destiny within a collaborative framework
- poverty and starvation would be largely eliminated through sharing and caring based on a process of empowering others
- development of people would be holistic with longer lifespans, a balanced life and multi-choice opportunities
- technology would be at a stage where it will have removed most of the limited skill or routine tasks
- organizations would be decentralized and designed to respond to local and community needs, in addition to fulfilling 'corporate' needs
- leadership in all walks of life would be concerned with empowering to ensure goals are realized through collaboration and synergy.

I have woven the strategic directions into a preferred scenario of the year 2000 and beyond. In constructing the scenario I have used a 'space structure' approach (Figure 2.2).

When visiting the 1976 Expo site in Montreal, I was impressed by the USA space structure based on Buckminster Fuller's Geodesic Dome concept. Its apparent simplicity yet great strength through its interconnecting framework left me wondering how we could use the concept to construct a similar framework to enable people to grow. The space structure concept has been central to my thinking as it provides an ideal analogy for the development of people.

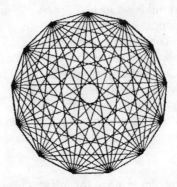

Figure 2.2   Representation of a space structure

The space structure represents the following:

- a 'whole person' approach to developing people through many avenues of learning and experience
- potential benefits to be derived from networking which allows us to share and exchange in an empowering manner
- a new approach to learning and development as it exemplifies multiple paths to learning in contrast to the current linear approach.

I am excited by the power of the space structure concept as it relates to us and the future. In choosing the architecture on which I should build any future scenario I use the polygon as my building block. This allows me to illustrate my ideas as units which integrate with others in a holistic model. Although each idea may appear discrete, it will in fact develop interdependent relationships with other ideas to create the whole (Figure 2.3).

The concepts of enabling leadership are contained in a pentagon shape which are combined to construct a larger pentagon. As we explore each concept the ideas which emerge form other pentagons thus creating an integrated space structure. The size and contents of each structure will depend on the unique needs and desires of each individual.

Using the results from a strategic thinking process, let us now examine my preferred scenario for the year 2000 and beyond.

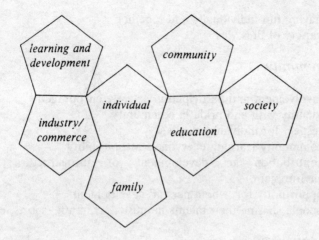

Figure 2.3   Components of an enabling environment

SCENARIO FOR THE YEAR 2000 AND BEYOND

The picture which emerges is an optimistic one. The following are the six main components of my future scenario:

Individual

- belief in and respect for self and others
- lifelong learner
- builds genuine relationships
- seeks win/win solutions
- collaborative
- achiever and contributor
- enjoys living

Family

- caring, sharing environment
- contribution based on ability and motivation
- freedom to grow with minimum dependency
- all contributing to learning and development
- genuine relationships

- having fun individually and together
- variety of lifestyles

Community

- involvement and participation actively encouraged
- identity with and pride in community
- respect for individual needs
- community learning everyone's responsibility
- contribution to development of infrastructure and environment
- opportunity for 'whole person' development
- people sharing their talents in music, art, crafts, sports, etc.

Organization

- collegiate management based on collaboration
- focus on developing people as means of creating profit
- open, trusting and consistent environment
- creativity encouraged
- involvement in decision making
- commitment to achievement
- rewards based on contribution
- concern for individual, family, community and society
- people enjoying involvement and making a contribution

Society

- caring and sharing
- collaborative
- individuals respected
- freedom with responsibility
- everyone involved in making a contribution – equality of worth
- win/win solutions sought
- having fun encouraged

Learning

- lifelong process
- home/community based

- collaborative resources with teachers, parents, community and industry
- multi-track/multi-vehicles
- learner-centred
- achievement encouraged through cooperation
- performance reviewed as continuous process
- individual and small-group learning designed to meet learning styles/needs
- 'whole person' development
- music, crafts, art, sports, meditation as integrated part of learning
- freedom to succeed (fail).

When we bring the blocks together, with a little artistic licence, we construct a polysphere which represents my vision of the year 2000 and beyond (Figure 2.4). The process involves enablers in developing structures which provide individuals with an opportunity to develop attitudes, skills and knowledge appropriate to

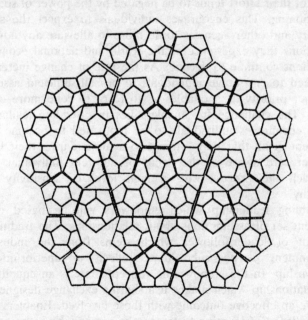

Figure 2.4   Vision of the World 2000

the contribution they can make. Although individuals have different abilities, the enabling environment allows each to develop and play their part in achieving results for the benefit of all.

The remainder of the book will focus on the people and the processes they can follow to realize a positive future in the years ahead. The people exist today and when they are energized they will form a powerful and positive force for change, based on a fundamental respect for the individual. I call these people 'enablers' and the process 'enabling leadership'.

ENABLING LEADERSHIP

Over the years, enablers have recognized the importance of creating a climate which encourages individuals to accept responsibility for their contribution to society. However, in some countries much of their effort tends to be negated by the power of societal conditioning. This encourages individuals to expect the state, industry and other agencies to do more to alleviate any adverse conditions they experience as the world and national economic conditions continue to decline. As the rate of change increases, the need to encourage individuals to be self-sufficient assumes a higher priority as it enables us to learn to cope more effectively. The challenge for enablers lies in providing leadership which encourages individuals to be motivated to become self-sufficient in all that they attempt to achieve during their lives. Enablers are aware of the needs of different individuals and approach the process with a high level of sensitivity and empathy.

Enabling leadership which empowers will be based on a different set of assumptions about relationships. The traditional concept of leader/follower which stems from the industrial environment of boss/subordinate reflects a superior/inferior relationship. In the empowering concept there is an equality in the relationship which makes it a sharing exchange designed to achieve an effective outcome with those involved. Enablers face the challenge of learning to transact in a manner which enables individuals to:

- understand their role in an organization and community
- be involved in establishing organizational and individual goals to which they are committed
- be committed to acquiring the attitudes, skills and knowledge to enable them to make an effective contribution
- accept responsibility for their own individual learning and development
- develop enabling relationships.

Building self-sufficiency provides individuals with confidence to tackle change with awareness of the possible consequences which can arise from each intended strategy/tactic.

This enabling leadership focus will be sharp and clear in that energy and skill will be devoted to raising awareness of how latent talent can best be released for the benefit of the individual and society. There will be many opportunities for enablers to accept the challenge and to provide empowering leadership. As we expand our thinking we learn to reshape our attitudes and thus develop an expanded portfolio of skills and knowledge. This will enable us to position ourselves to offer effective leadership now and in the future.

As time evolves and scenarios change, we shall be ideally positioned to recognize new indicators thus offering us the opportunity to continue to shaping a society which offers hope, opportunity and fulfilment to all. This is the positive future I predict will emerge as enabling leadership provides the key to releasing the talent latent within most of us. How this can be achieved is described in detail in Part II.

3 Overview of enabling leadership

The more I am involved in working with people in different types of organization around the world the more certain I become of the need for us to view leadership from a new perspective which I call enabling leadership. In the previous chapter I projected a future scenario whilst indicating the challenge which faces enablers in shaping a positive world. In this chapter I draw a profile of enabling leadership and outline its components. These are explored in depth in Parts II and III. As you read this book I believe that you will begin to build a picture of how enabling leadership can realize an exciting future for us all.

THE EMERGING ENABLER

A new type of person has been emerging over recent years, a person who is able to think about issues and express ideas and opinions designed to improve; who cares, not only about him/herself but also about others, the community and society. This caring is expressed in all that they do and say and can be seen in the sensitive and enabling behaviours they use with others. The fact that enabling leaders are emerging in many countries suggests that enabling can be a part of each of us wherever we live. It will be practised in different ways appropriate to each culture. The only constraint will be whether the environment encourages it to be overtly or covertly practised. Whatever the situation most people who want to enable have the capacity to do so, and actually do so in their own ways.

Therefore as I describe enabling leadership I hope that you will see there are many ways to be an enabling leader. Enabling leadership has been with us for a long time but has been suppressed by our industrial society. As we move rapidly to the new information and high-tech society we can see a climate emerging which requires enabling leadership.

It is also important to note that the new breed of enabling people is not restricted to a particular class or section of a particular society. Such people are emerging from all classes of society and are distinguished by their personal philosophy which guides their lives and motivates them. To provide a sharper picture of enabling leadership and the role of an enabler, I have prepared the following definitions:

Enabling leadership

- Enabling leadership is a process whereby all the people involved in achieving a goal or outcome are able to contribute in an effective manner. Their contribution is released through an understanding of what each individual has to do, coupled with readiness to do more, to see the goal accomplished. Leadership is inherent in the team and passes from one person to another as the situation requires. The enabling process provides an environment which encourages everyone to contribute to achieve results.

An enabler

- An enabler is a person who operates from a philosophy of empowering which enables him or her to relate to others in a way which generates synergy. Enablers are sensitive and aware and strive to improve their effectiveness in terms of their own personal contribution. Enabling others to help themselves is one of their main aims as they recognize that by building confidence in others, competence has a high possibility of emerging. The output of their efforts can be measured in the way they achieve results with people.

When I use the term enabler, I mean a person who practises enabling leadership. To provide a framework for exploring enabling leadership I have developed a model with six components which are fitted together to represent an integrated whole (Figure 3.1).

I have again used the concept of the space structure to illustrate the interconnecting nature of the six components of enabling leadership. The first three, Enabling Awareness, Enabling Philosophy and Enabling Learning, concern the development of the enabler and are the components which shape the person. The other three, Enabling Roles, Enabling Process and Enabling Change, concern the what and how of the practice of enabling leadership by the enabler. To illustrate the part each component contributes to Enabling Leadership, I shall now briefly describe them:

ENABLING AWARENESS

Awareness is central to the development of enabling leadership. It includes awareness of self, others and of the environments

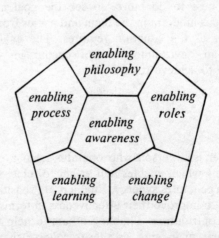

Figure 3.1   Enabling leadership model

within which we operate. As belief in self is the foundation on which the enabler's philosophy is built, it is imperative that we develop the skills to understand ourselves. In addition we need to know the effect we have on others, and why.

Awareness is generally taken for granted as most of us believe we understand ourselves. It can come as a shock when, on occasions, we receive feedback on how others see us which produces a starkly contrasting picture to our own view. This feeling is often allowed to dissipate quickly and we continue life unaffected. However, to be an enabler we have a responsibility to take ourselves seriously and have a genuine desire to understand the effect we have on those with whom we interact.

Gaining this understanding can be an enriching experience as it provides us with insights which help us relate more effectively. There are many vehicles and techniques to learn and know ourselves better. These often illustrate how our perception differs from that of others; feedback provides us with ideas on how we can learn to modify our behaviour to meet the real needs of other people.

Enablers develop a sensitivity to detect the feedback being continuously transmitted by people with whom they interact both directly and indirectly. Having a desire to understand ourselves leads us to seek feedback and also show an interest in what is happening around us. As we develop our awareness and learn to understand what drives us to think and behave the way we do, we also learn to recognize what drives other people. Our awareness provides us with an understanding of others and a growing realization that little will be achieved until we meet their needs. Once their needs have been met they in turn will be ready and willing to meet our needs. This is one of the keys to achieving results with people and obtaining synergistic relationships.

On the broader front, we also need to raise our awareness to enable us to understand what is happening at home, work and play. Each situation is an environment in its own right, with its own special culture or mix of cultures. Developing our natural curiosity will lead us to a greater sense of what is going on in the world around us, be it on a micro or macro-scale. Being in touch with ourselves and our environment can provide us with a sense of purpose and direction which feeds our belief system and leads to greater confidence in all that we do and say. We are motivated to learn about our philosophy, how it influences what we are as a person and our interactions with others in different contexts.

The same can be said about our awareness of business environments. Once we have identified the organization's strategic directions and decoded its culture, we can check whether it corresponds with our own philosophy. Any variations which conflict with our value system may indicate where our enabling intervention starts. Alternatively, it may indicate that we are investing our talents in the wrong place.

Enabling means that we need to understand how we can develop ourselves to be effective and thus be more capable when we interact with others in different environments. Helping others is understood and accepted by enablers to be an empowering process. As our awareness is raised, we can recognize how the process can be employed to ensure that it creates positive results. These results will be achieved mainly by the way we relate to others, a process which is driven by our personal value system.

ENABLING PHILOSOPHY

Enabling is a conscious process of interacting with others to empower them to achieve results using individual and collective talents. Relationships are based on a genuine desire to understand each other and release potential to produce solutions which result in the desired achievement.

As I meet and interact with enablers it becomes obvious that they are guided by a strong personal philosophy which embraces the following values:

- self-responsibility
- belief and respect for self and others
- open and build trust
- willing to share in a caring manner
- build relationships on a genuine basis
- aim to empower others
- results oriented with a vision of the future.

Each person develops his/her own mix of components to meet his/her individual needs. However, observations clearly indicate that enablers tend to adopt most of these values.

Having a strong belief in yourself is the foundation on which an enabling philosophy is built. It is based on an awareness and understanding of our potential according to the skills, knowledge and attitudes we possess. Awareness is a continually developing process which is at the heart of enabling leadership.

Having a clear picture of our strengths and areas of future development means that we can improve our performance and relate to others in an effective manner. Relationships are thus seen as the way to achieve results with others. The magnetic attraction of the effectiveness of 'synergy' provides the energy to work at creating effective relationships. Enablers seek to build relationships in a genuine manner avoiding ulterior motives. The uniqueness of individuals is recognized and it is understood that sound relationships are based on meeting mutual needs.

Working to achieve win/win solutions at all times provides the stimulus to see issues from the other person's viewpoint. The enabler is guided by a desire to achieve results which gain the commitment of all involved. This generally ensures that the subsequent activity is carried out within agreed terms. Win/win solutions are exciting to discover as they often provide unique ways to help others. The enabler's drive to empower is based on an awareness that commitment will be gained if the solution seeker owns the solution.

The aim of the enabler is to work to develop an environment which encourages people to be solution-seekers, with an ability to translate their solution into results. The vision of the enabler is to empower others to achieve on a self-help basis, whilst recognizing when and how other people can help. Living out one's philosophy comes from deep conviction and confidence in oneself which is continually strengthened through increasing awareness.

Through all that enablers do flows the understanding of how much responsibility rests with them to ensure that relationships are genuine and legitimate. The self-responsibility component is a factor in guiding enablers in all that they may do when working with people. Their aim will be to display their own responsibility thus encouraging others to take responsibility for their own thoughts and actions.

Being a responsible person provides a sound basis on which to build and develop enabling skills. It also provides a strong motivation to be abreast of current developments and to acquire and practise new skills. Irrespective of the mix of components of philosophy an enabler lives by, there is an inherent respect for self and others. There is also a real awareness of the need to develop and thus being an active learner is an integrated part of their belief system.

ENABLING LEARNING

By now an emerging awareness of what enabling learning entails should embrace an understanding of the need to view learning as a continuous and lifelong process.

An enabling leader believes in and practises lifelong learning. Being a continuous learner means always being ready to learn at every opportunity and from every interaction with others. Being convinced of the value of lifelong learning provides enablers with the desire to be effective in constructing learning opportunities for themselves and others.

They are aware of the value of learning from experience and seek to find ways for all to benefit. Learning will be achieved in different ways depending on our individual learning styles and preferences. Enablers will be aware that there are many different components to the construction of effective learning environments.

One important function of the enabler is to create a learning environment which encourages individual learners to be responsible for their own development. Enablers will understand that this may take time as some individuals will be very dependent on others at an early stage. They will be weaned from dependency by building their confidence as they transfer learning into daily practice.

Enablers work to develop the following when constructing an effective learning environment:

- developmental climate
- learning expectations/goals
- learning contact
- accountability
- awareness of learning styles
- effective learning transfer
- appropriate learning assistance.

Responsibility and accountability will be encouraged through individuals gaining a clear understanding of what they expect and want to learn. Being clear about learning expectations is a vital part of the learning process. It enables us to think about what we expect to achieve and express this as our learning goals. Each learning goal will be observable and measurable and will provide us with a vision of what we are aiming to achieve. Once we have gained the desired end result, we also know that we have succeeded.

Having clear learning goals enables individuals to identify how and where learning can take place and who may be involved. When other individuals are required to assist in the learning process, the learner can explain what is expected from them. In many instances the contribution from the other person is expressed in an oral or written learning agreement. Although not intended as a legal document, this does have a powerful moral value. Firstly, it places the main responsibility with the learner and secondly, it shows others the importance the learner places on their contribution. A learning agreement is useful in illustrating that obligations are placed on all parties to see agreed contributions are fulfilled.

An enabler will be aware of the different learning styles which individuals have acquired. Learning design will take account of individual learning styles and preferences as a means of facilitating the learning process. Individual learners will also be encouraged to understand their preferences with a view to experiencing other styles and extending their range of learning approaches. The stage can be reached where individuals can select and construct the most appropriate learning approaches to meet their specific needs for each learning goal. This will allow them to use many of the existing provisions with a full awareness of what they expect to achieve.

Effective transfer of learning is the door through which all learners must pass if learning is recognized as relevant. The key to opening the door lies in being aware, self-managed learners, selecting appropriate vehicles of learning with an increasing sensitivity to the implications of the acquisition of new skills and attitudes in daily practice.

Most of us will need help to develop ourselves as we break out of the sequential and linear process to which we have become accustomed.The space structure concept illustrates that there are many ways to learn and many avenues to take. Enablers believe in looking for the whole picture and then filling in the detail as they progress through the lifelong learning process. Help will be available and will be willingly given by enablers on the clear understanding that it is designed to empower.

Being involved in an open and multi-path learning environment allows the enabler to build awareness and develop a personal philosophy which meets the mission of empowering others and themselves. They can also identify and acquire the attitudes, skills and knowledge (ASK) associated with enabling leadership. The acronym ASK is a useful reminder of the responsibility we have to others to ask them to assist us whilst providing a clear picture of what is sought and the groundrules under which it can be contributed.

Viewing every solution as a learning opportunity stimulates the enabler to seek to make positive use of appropriate events. This may be for personal learning, to develop awareness or receive feedback on the use of a newly acquired, or further developed skill. Being aware of the many opportunities to learn provides motivation to continue to improve and develop. It is this wish to be a continuous learner, as a means of improving effectiveness, which defines another cornerstone of the enabling leader.

Enablers integrate the foundation components of awareness, philosophy and learning to form a set of values and beliefs which influence all that they do. We recognize the power of the knowing/doing syndrome and understand that the benefits of enabling need to be observed in action. Part II takes us into the arena of outputs from enabling leadership.

ENABLING OUTPUTS

The key benefits derived from enabling leadership can be observed in how enablers construct environments which result in individuals being involved, committed and productive. The three main parts which contribute to enabling outputs are:

- enabling roles
- enabling process
- enabling change.

We shall see that enabling roles are effective vehicles for achieving outputs which are beneficial and also play a significant part in enabling change. The link between roles and change is the enabling process which allows the quality of outputs to be enhanced. Enabling process focuses on two main components – enabling organizations and enabling contributions – which when integrated provide the basis for synergistic achievment. When created, enabling organizations provide a real opportunity for individuals to make their contribution. In enabling contribution we examine what enablers do to encourage individuals to be effective.

ENABLING ROLES

When thinking about the skills used in enabling leadership, it was interesting to note that they were primarily process skills. If you examine the description of enabling leadership outlined to this point, you will realize that the skills are clustered in such a way that they describe the following roles:

- understanding communicator
- developmental counsellor
- coach and mentor
- solution seeker
- achiever and orchestrator.

Most of these roles are process-oriented and are concerned with empowering others. Being aware of the need to work towards empowering others to feel good about achieving by using their own resources requires active listening, communication and solution-seeking skills. Enabling will naturally include operating from a counselling mode to encourage others to think through the issues.

Once an appropriate solution has been found, and the person concerned has 'bought it', an action plan can be developed. It is quite probable that the person may need help and this can be provided through a coaching or mentor relationship. At all times the enabler concentrates on helping others acquire the confidence, skills, knowledge and motivation to accomplish the goal through their own efforts where this is appropriate.

It is stimulating to observe that there are an increasing number of people adapting their style to use many of the enabling roles described. They recognize that commitment and motivation come from actively involving people in the decision-making process, particularly on issues which directly affect them. The environment is constructed to empower individuals to feel competent and able to shape their contribution to achieve the organization's goals and at the same time fulfil their own goals.

Finding ways to help a person solve a problem or take advantage of an opportunity can be a demanding responsibility. It is much less of a problem when the person is determined to seek a solution which fits the need. However, when the person is not motivated, for whatever reason, to seek a solution we have a quite different set of circumstances.

The enabler will assess each situation to determine how the person is approaching the issue. Although there is no one set of responses which will meet all situations, there are a number of criteria we can use to help us.

ENABLING PROCESS (1) – ENABLING ORGANIZATION

We use the term 'organization' to describe a person's interface with one or more environments, such as home, work, school, club, sports team, etc. Any interface with others will involve us as part of an 'organization' which will influence or be influenced in the process. As we briefly examine the criteria we can explore their relationship to a business organization as a way of illustrating how they can relate to our personal 'organizations'.

An organization which has a clear mission will find that it can achieve its desired result whilst providing its people with satisfaction and even fulfilment. If people feel good about their organization, know what is expected of them and how they can go about what is required, the chances are high that they will achieve. That is why it is important to encourage individuals to identify their goal and to ensure that the environment enhances their motivation.

The term 'culture' is increasingly used to describe an organization. Cultures comprises a set of values which are shared by its
members. One of the stimulating benefits of organizational
cultural analysis is in the identification of those values which tend
to enhance its members' motivation. Identifying these components
gives us a map of how to effect change in the most effective
manner. The same principal applies to us as individuals in that
it is vital to identify those personal values, from the relevant
environment, which are essential in helping us to achieve our
desired goals.

Team working provides opportunities for individuals to
contribute from their portfolio of skills and knowledge in a manner
which adds value to the expected output. One of the bonuses of
team working is achieving synergy: i.e. the output realized is
greater than the sum of the individual effort contributed. Working
in a team can be an exciting developmental process as we can
gain a great deal by learning from each other. This is one reason
why enablers encourage individuals to be part of teams. If we
could only learn to be effective team members, the effect on our
lives would be impressive and full of potential for our personal
development.

ENABLING PROCESS (2) – ENABLING CONTRIBUTION

It is vital to be conscious of what we are aiming to achieve. Having
a clear goal which we can visualize completed, is a good starting
point. Describing our goals in terms of their desired outcome is
vital to achievement. The vision is more likely to become a reality
as we begin to work towards achieving it, and as it take shape we
shall use the skills and knowledge required. If others are involved,
we shall agree the roles they will adopt to enable us to achieve
our goal. With everyone working towards the same goal and
understanding what they need to do, progress is more rapid. That
is where working as a team can release peoples energy in creative
ways to fulfil our own and the organization's goals.

Another benefit is the availability of objective feedback on
performance. Given that the goals are expressed in measurable,
observable and understandable terms, the process of feedback on

performance can be agreed. It makes a great deal of sense to arrange for feedback on performance to be given. Most of us learn from trying to do something and seeing the results of our efforts. We can modify what we do and thus improve on our previous performance. Receiving feedback is essential to our learning and it is one of the key elements of enabling leadership. However, like many of the things we do, it has to be handled in an appropriate and effective way. We need to be able to draw on our portfolio of skills, knowledge and attitudes which enables us to achieve the desired outcomes.

We can draw the criteria together to present a picture of enabling leaders working through a series of actions to encourage an individual, or group, to construct a process, or set of processes, to enable their goals to be realized. The fundamental aim of the enabler is to develop in those involved the confidence to recognize where they want to go, develop their mission, acquire and use the appropriate skills, link with others as required and move forward to achieve their goals. By 'owning' the process they will be responsible and motivated to achieve.

Accepting the need to continue to improve performance is an essential part of an enabler's philosophy. It makes enablers want to be as effective as possible and thus be competent in the way they contribute their skills and knowledge to whatever they do. Through commitment to achieve and empower enablers will wish to acquire and develop their enabling skills. Building competence in the use of enabling skills provides us with the ability to cope with change wherever we meet it.

ENABLING CHANGE

Coping with change is one of the most important challenges facing us today and will continue to be so in the future. That is why enabling leadership will become a significant means to facing all change in a positive and constructive manner.

As we strive to be effective enablers, we shall be faced with situations which may require us to change our attitudes, behaviour, appearance, approach, manner, skills and knowledge. Awareness of what change is and how to manage the process provides us with the possibility of accomplishing it successfully. If we live by an enabling philosophy, we shall approach the change process as follows:

- recognize that change starts within us
- aim to understand the change process
- adopt a positive attitude to change
- decide where our intervention would be most effective
- accept change as inevitable and thus work at enabling ourselves and others to 'manage' it for our mutual benefit.

Agreeing that change has to start with ourselves is one of the keys to learning to cope and adapt to each situation which is affected by change. Enablers recognize the need for enabling change as a process of equipping ourselves in an effective manner to meet the external factors causing us to change. They understand the process of change and how it impacts on individuals, how it can disable people through its bewildering complexity and how it can be harnessed for positive outcomes.

Another issue is the attitude we adopt to change. We have a choice. We can see it as a threat to which we react by defending the status quo and then risking the danger of entering, and being locked into, a defensive cycle of behaviours. Alternatively, we can see it as an opportunity and approach it with anticipation and enthusiasm within a development cycle which encourages us to make the best possible use of the change. Adopting a development cycle approach enables us to approach the need for change with confidence.

We shall see the challenge of change as a chance to develop rather than as a problem. Our attitude will form part of our philosophy and permeate all that we do and say. People will be able to relate to us and through our enabling we shall encourage them to contribute in a willingly manner. As the fear of change is replaced by positive anticipation of how we can manage its effects, we gain in confidence. And as we become more confident our self-image improves and we build up a belief in ourselves.

SUMMARY

Enabling leadership is about self-leadership. It is about taking responsibility for our lives in a way which shows sensitivity to our needs as well as the needs of others. We seek to develop ourselves in a way which improves our ability to be effective. Through this we learn to relate to others as individuals or as team members with the aim of accomplishing results. As our words and actions are congruent, people learn to trust us and feel able to interact with us in an open and collaborative manner. Synergy results and the problems of change are tackled with vigour, determination and with the confidence of eventual success.

Enabling leadership releases the talent and motivation of all involved and encourages us to have a vision of what we want to accomplish. It also creates an environment within which we shall work to make it materialize. The benefits will eventually be shared with society in general as enabling leadership furnishes the people and process to solve many of the world's problems. I have this vision and I believe that it will happen . . . in the near future.

Part II
FOUNDATION OF ENABLING

Explores the three key components in developing as an enabling leader

CONCEPTS EXPLORED IN CHAPTER 4

AWARENESS MODEL
SELF-AWARENESS
   Need for Self-Awareness
   Steps to Interpersonal Skill Development
   Understanding Behaviour
   Interpersonal Choice
SELF-AWARENESS PROCESS
   Unique Journey
   Opening Doors to Understanding
   Learning from Others
   Our Predictable Self
   Travelling Light
   Influence of Culture
AWARENESS OF OTHERS
   Historical Awareness
   Trust in Relationships
   Managing Relationships
ENVIRONMENTAL AWARENESS
   Describing an Organization
   Exploring an Environment
   Test Assumptions
   Scanning the Environment
   Strategic Signposts
   Confronting Assumptions
   Strategic Directions
   USING AWARENESS

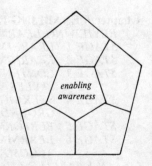

enabling awareness

4 Enabling awareness

Interacting with enablers is a satisfying experience owing to their ability to understand others' needs and their knowledge of how to enable others to accomplish whatever they set out to do. An enabler's ability to sense what action is required provides a framework of confidence which allows a transaction to be conducted in a positive manner. When the issues are sensitive or could generate hostility and conflict, the enabler uses processes which encourage the participants to concentrate on the 'reality' of the issues and draw away from the emotional arena. Enablers have a wonderful skill in being able to chart paths through a wide variety of situations and to lead those involved, without being dogmatic or directive. Individuals feel that they are free to contribute to the issue and usually do so in a mannter which results in a win/win situation for all concerned. The outcome is usually one from which participants emerge with a feeling of being empowered by the experience.

Through recognizing the power of enabling, I was encouraged to explore in more depth the way enablers operate. I wanted to understand their knowledge and skills and how they knew what to use and when. A recurring theme emerged which could be described as the way they had developed their antennae to 'sense' what was happening during interpersonal transactions. Enablers were able to assess a situation and know what to do to achieve a positive and appropriate conclusion. From further research, a picture emerged of how enablers had developed their 'antennae' and how it was a continually growing process.

We discovered that the process began with enablers developing a need to be aware of themselves in the sense of understanding how their behaviour impacted on others. This is the starting point: for many it is a gradual process as they 'discover' themselves as awareness grows, whereas for others the trigger was a traumatic incident. Incidents ranged from unexpected and unwarranted pleasure and gratitude being expressed, to attitudes of resentment, anger and hostility – again without apparent cause being given by an enabler. The outcome of particular transactions resulted in enablers being taken by surprise by the attitude and behaviour of those involved. The initial response tended to be to rationalize the situation to fit their individual perception, followed by further thoughts as the answer still left some uncertainty. So enablers started to examine what they said and did during transactions and began to build awareness of the specific behaviours which triggered particular responses from people in general and some individuals in particular.

The way in which enablers acquired their awareness was as unique as each individual enabler. However, if we can accept the principle that it is possible to learn from others, it allows us the scope to pull together the various ideas and present them within a framework. My intention is to set a framework of awareness which indicates the many routes which can be taken to acquire a competent level. I approach the task aware and sensitive to the challenge enabling leadership presents.

I perceive my role as an architect offering ideas on the building blocks with suggestions on how you may put them together and the benefits which can accrue. Yet I also accept that each reader may have a different set of perceptions which motivates them to construct quite different shapes. The important issue is not the shape but the outcome of the building and development in terms of empowering the individual to empower others in an enabling manner.

AWARENESS MODEL

The process has three distinct yet integrated components which provide a sound framework which the enabler can work on. In terms of enabling leadership this involves us developing the following three components of awareness.

- Self-awareness – an awareness of self and how this enables us to understand and accept ourselves; to learn to understand what makes us act and behave the way we do and the effect this has on others
- Awareness of others – from a developed self-awareness we shall be better equipped to understand and thus behave in a manner which allows us to relate more effectively with others; through understanding and being willing to meet their needs to achieve win/win outcomes
- Environmental awareness – how to use our self-awareness to develop skills to interpret the various environments in which we are involved or have an interest.

SELF-AWARENESS

Self-awareness is a state of personal awareness which enables us to interpret and understand the values, beliefs and attitudes we hold and how these influence our behaviour and its impact on others. As we explore the concepts and techniques of developing self-awareness we should realize that its primary aim is to equip us with an understanding of ourselves. Through our developing awareness and understanding we identify the knowledge, skills and attitudes which will enable us to obtain the best results from our interpersonal transactions.

Self-awareness will influence all aspects of our thinking and provide a framework to think through any activity which has an outcome affecting another person. When we write or prepare to speak, it will be done in an enabling manner with awareness of its potential impact on the recipient. When we see that our actions and behaviour are creating an impact which is inappropriate, we are able to modify them to transform the transaction to achieve positive results.

Need for self-awareness

Let us examine why self-awareness is prerequisite to achieving effective and rewarding relationships. Each person sees and interprets the world according to his/her 'mind set' or 'frame of reference'. This has been developed through the conditioning and experiences of life and is part of their attitude, value and belief system. This means that people 'judge' their own behaviour and that of others with a 'conditioned' mind, ear and eye. It is the recognition that each of us is unique in the way we see and interpret what is going on that makes the process of self-awareness central to operating effectively.

We realize that what we 'see' is our perception based on our conditioning and that others also 'see' situations in their own unique way. It is by first gaining a perspective on our conditioning that we are able to understand why we think and feel as we do. Then, with an open mind, testing our perceptions with those of others will enable us to work towards achieving mutual understanding with an awareness of how our behaviour is perceived. Without this focus and recognition of what influences us, we are left unaware of how our behaviour affects the people we interact with. It is worth noting that situations in which we interact with others include:

- face-to-face meetings at which our involvement can range from being in charge to a more supporting role
- meetings which we attend as a participant/spectator
- communications by telephone and in writing
- any situation in which our presence (or absence) will affect relationships.

The more we become aware of the variety of ways in which we influence relationships, the better able we shall be to understand how to act to achieve positive outcomes. Recognizing that what we project in direct relationships is also supported by perceptions and inputs from many indirect sources is crucial. This reinforces the view of how we as individuals fit into a wide network of relationships. The impression we create in one situation, is likely to be communicated to others. Thus we have the ripple effect like dropping a pebble into a pool, the result of which (planned or otherwise), will wash up in someone's mind sooner or later.

Steps to interpersonal skill development

Understanding the vulnerability of the multi-channel process of communicating ourselves through our behaviour is an important initial step in self-awareness. To illustrate this, it is useful to relate it to two models which explain some aspects of our behaviour. The first model (Figure 4.1) involves the stages of interpersonal skill development and indicates four steps which we can take to improve our interpersonal skills.

The lowest level of skill is illustrated as a negative in that people who operate as unconscious incompetents are unaware of the disabling effects of their behaviour on others. They appear to operate as unguided missiles who hit a target with the effect of an interpersonal *Exocet*. Neither the target nor the effect is planned nor is the person aware of the often devastating effect.

From research we identified how simple it is to operate as an unconscious incompetent when our awareness is low and we have not thought through what we are doing. Once we become aware of the negative effect of our behaviour we move on to the next step of being a conscious incompetent. We now have a glimmer of awareness which tells us that all is not well in our transactions. The results are examined and the causes understood. This step offers us the choice of continuing as we are or modifying our behaviour.

If we choose the latter course, we identify the areas of skill, knowledge and attitudes necessary to equip us to operate more effectively. As we acquire a level of effectiveness, we move on to the third level of conscious competent which is the basic level of performance in interpersonal skills. At this level we begin to understand what we are doing and what the outcomes may be. We continue to develop our awareness and practise interpersonal skills and reach the top step of unconscious competent by being able to perform, when interacting, on 'autopilot'.

Our antennae are well developed as we increasingly understand our behaviour and internalize how to achieve positive outcomes from all our interactions. Just as we need to practise to maintain

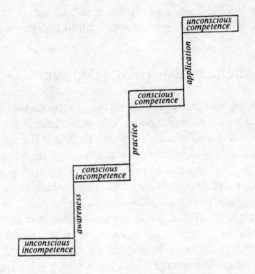

Figure 4.1　Steps to interpersonal skill development

a satisfactory standard in the performance of any skill, the same principle applies to interpersonal skills. The model clearly indicates the responsibility we have in learning to understand our behaviour and its effect on others to enable us to modify it to achieve positive outcomes.

Understanding behaviour

Understanding behaviour can be a fascinating and exciting activity. It often resembles unravelling a mystery plot in a good detective novel. As we think we have reached a point of understanding a significant part of what triggers behavioural responses, further evidence appears which leads us off in another direction. Learning about behaviours involves a process of unwrapping the layers of experience and knowledge to understand more about what drives us as individuals. We use the 'onion' as the second model (Figure 4.2) to represent this unwrapping to get at the core of ourselves.

At the core we have clusters of beliefs which shape the values we hold. We draw on these values when we encounter situations and they help shape our attitudes. Our values and beliefs are continually being formed and reshaped throughout our lives. Much of the input into shaping and reshaping our values and beliefs is acquired unconsciously through observation and experience. The first we learn about a particular value comes when we react violently to some stimulus, after which we are surprised, if not shocked, by the depth of feeling surrounding the incident.

As input is continuous and influenced by environment and culture, our conditioning is powerfully reinforced by experience. If, for example, we value honesty and we are involved in a situation which challenges this value, our response will be shaped by the depth of feeling we hold about honesty coupled with our perceptions and expectations of how we should react in the particular environment.

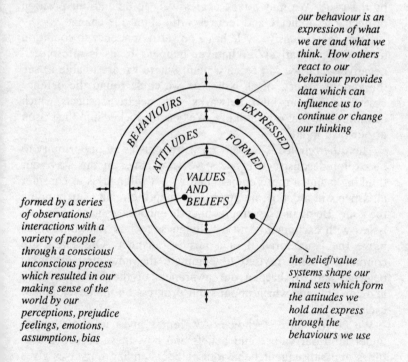

our behaviour is an expression of what we are and what we think. How others react to our behaviour provides data which can influence us to continue or change our thinking

formed by a series of observations/ interactions with a variety of people through a conscious/ unconscious process which resulted in our making sense of the world by our perceptions, prejudice feelings, emotions, assumptions, bias

the belief/value systems shape our mind sets which form the attitudes we hold and express through the behaviours we use

Figure 4.2   Onion of behaviour

Interpersonal choice

To expand on the question of how our attitudes are shaped by experience and environment, we developed the following interpersonal choice model (Figure 4.3). This shows that when we are involved in thinking about a response to a stimulus (issue), we can react positively or negatively. The choice we make is influenced by the attitudes we hold and whether these influence us to perceive the issue as a threat or opportunity. If the perception is one of threat, the route we follow is to enter a defensive cycle with our attitudes being shaped to retain the status quo. To achieve this we enter a defensive mode expressed through behaviours which show that we are unwilling to accept change. Defensive behaviour displays our fear, uncertainty and the fact that we feel threatened by the issue. We may attack aggressively to defend our position or decide to abdicate and feel resentful about the change.

Being in a defensive cycle has a powerful tendency to condition us to think negatively. Whatever happens to us is interpreted negatively and we can reach a point where we are unable to see the various aspects of an issue. As we circle round the defence cycle, we fill our filter networks with negative aspects which condition and bias our thinking. We become locked into the prison of our own minds.

The other choice is to view each stimulus as an opportunity to be explored constructively. As we view issues in this way, our thinking is much more open-ended with a willingness to consider all aspects in a deliberate attempt to map the reality surrounding the issue. Being in a development cycle encourages us to approach issues with excitement and a willingness to find solutions which move the issue forward in a positive manner. Our filters are continually being revised to eliminate the unwanted historical baggage and to sharpen our awareness of the bias, prejudice and conditioning which impairs our progress on the development cycle.

We clearly have a choice. Awareness gives us the tools to understand our values and beliefs and how these influence attitudes and subsequent behaviour. Understanding ourselves gives us a basis on which we can begin to understand what drives others to act and behave as they do. Clearing our filters is the prominent thrust in self-awareness. The process requires us to begin to under-

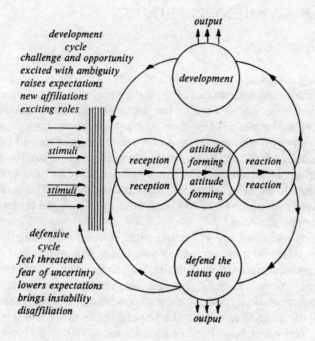

development
cycle
challenge and opportunity
excited with ambiguity
raises expectations
new affiliations
exciting roles

stimuli

stimuli

defensive
cycle
feel threatened
fear of uncertinty
lowers expectations
brings instability
disaffiliation

Figure 4.3 Interpersonal choice model

stand what makes us tick and how this influences us to act and react when confronted by stimuli of all kinds.

Being aware of whether the thoughts which condition us are positive or negative enables us to take appropriate action. If we believe that our cause is better served by being in the defensive cycle, then that is the choice we would make. On the other hand, if we believe that we ought to change and adapt to situations, we shall choose to be on the development cycle. Enablers continually strive to be on the development cycle as their ability to empower is enhanced through their ability to view the world and its working from an open and aware position.

SELF-AWARENESS PROCESS

Unique journey

Having accepted the necessity and with it the desire, to improve our self-awareness, we can explore the process and develop a plan which enables us to acquire the necessary attitudes, knowledge and skills. We aim to offer ideas on what are the necessary insights to understand who we are and how this influences us and others. The ideas are offered as signposts which point in one or more directions of development we can follow. However, the path we take has to be selected to meet our unique needs. The first step involves being motivated to learn about ourselves and understand what makes us 'tick'.

Being aware of the effect our attitudes and behaviour has on others is an essential part of self-awareness. When developing our awareness we must recognize that we are in a process of constant change. As we journey through life, change takes place in a combination of physical, social and psychological ways. Normally much of the change tends to be imperceptible as we live our lives with people who have become accustomed to our ways. However, this can be quite different when some event or incident suddenly puts us under the microscope. In these situations we are often confronted with perceptions of how much we have changed and how this affects other people.

There is often great comfort in learning from friends we have not seen for some time that we are looking good and have not changed. Our self-image is enhanced and we feel good about retaining our youth and vigour – or whatever it is we want to believe. It is a quite different story when we are confronted with the feedback that we are getting older, and are less fit, less energetic, or fatter than we thought. Self-awareness is very much about understanding how we change and being in control as much as possible. If we feel 21 inside at the age of 60, the young feeling will be expressed in many appropriate ways, but not by activities which are outside the realistic scope of the person. The ability to keep on testing new frontiers will keep us in good shape, accepting what we can do by mapping reality which keeps us in a development cycle.

To enable us to become aware we have to build a picture of

ourselves against which we can test the difference between our perceptions and those of others. It comes as a surprise to some people to learn that their self-concept can be projected in a manner which others perceive in quite a different form from that desired.

When we look into a mirror we usually see what we expect to see. If we feel tired, we see a tired person. If we feel healthy, slim and fit, that is how we see ourselves. The mirror will not only project a reverse image of who is placed in front of it, it will also be largely influenced by the attitude of those looking into it. Here is one of the keys to self-awareness. Seeing ourselves only through our own eyes has the danger of producing a distorted picture. In fact, this is the type of setting which traps us into operating as unconscious incompetents. Avoiding this route involves us in accepting the need to test our perceptions of what we are and project, with those on the receiving end. Getting behind the mirror requires us to be actively involved in a disclosure and feedback process.

Opening doors to understanding

Before we can start the feedback process, it is useful to think about the arena within which we seek understanding. It may be that we seek general feedback on how we appear to others in a wide variety of settings. Alternatively, we may seek feedback in one area of our behaviour. From our experience considerable benefits can initially derive from a narrow focus when starting to obtain feedback on our behaviour. Once we gain experience and confidence in handling feedback, we can widen the focus.

One useful technique involves identifying the area in which we seek feedback. For example, if we would like a better understanding of how we project ourselves when greeting people, we could think of several recent critical incidents of this kind. Thinking about the incidents, we could list the behaviours on which we would appreciate feedback. The following example illustrates what could emerge:

- because I feel uncertain, I believe that I project this to others by the tentative way I approach them

- when uncertain, my handshake tends to be limp and leaves me feeling unsure of how the other person feels about this and what they think of me
- I feel better when I sit behind my desk and let my secretary bring people in to me; then I stand and greet them. I sometimes feel that this does not help the subsequent transaction
- I know my forehead and hands are perspiring when I meet strangers and thus avoid shaking hands if I can
- I like to grasp my visitors' hands warmly and use my other hand to grasp their arm. Sometimes I feel that this friendly and open gesture is not welcomed.

The aim is to be as specific as possible in describing what we do, how we feel before, during and after the event. As we begin to describe the behaviours in observable/measurable terms we can set up a sound basis from which we can receive feedback. The next step requires us to think of some of the people who are involved in these critical incidents and select those who we feel would be able to give us feedback without its adversely affecting our relationship. Most people are willing and reasonably able to express their views when the feedback is requested against specific behaviours. A relatively non-threatening environment for both parties can be created by sharing our desire for an understanding of how we are perceived with selected individuals, and asking for their comments.

Having identified the area, found some critical incidents and listed the behaviours involved, we are well on the way to developing awareness. As we list the behaviours involved, we have the opportunity to think about the values and beliefs which influenced the underlying attitudes. We can also explore our perception of the attitudes which could be held by the people from whom we seek the feedback.

Learning from others

Receiving feedback gives us data which enable us to make modifications to our behaviour to meet the needs of others. Feedback can come in many different ways and is available if we learn to observe and seek it from others. As the self-awareness skills are developed we become more able to position our antennae to pick up the signals which are being transmitted. As we develop trust in others we are able to increase the empathy of the relationship and, through this, tune into the feedback wavelength of those people involved. All feedback needs to be processed to ensure that we understand its meaning and how it might affect us.

Testing perceptions can then come in the form of disclosures to other persons of what we perceive our impact is on them and/or on other individuals. This can take place at most times and will tend to be effective when we have secure relationships based on agreed ground rules. Although feedback can be more easily received from people in solid relationships it is also possible to develop ground rules which enable comparative strangers to provide feedback. Because of the trust and openness which the enabler communicates, people can feel secure in being open and frank with the feedback they provide.

Our predictable self

Throughout our life we develop a process of doing things in well-defined ways. This is part of our ability to make complex processes such as walking, cycling and swimming, simple. It allows us to develop unconscious routines for many parts of our daily life, thus releasing our mind to concentrate on other issues. It is a process which helps us to live our lives in an effective manner and thus releases our minds to work on the more complex issues of living in a rapidly changing world.

Developing routines to cover many aspects of our daily lives provides a framework which allows others to get to know us. Their understanding is generally based on observations of what we do and say in various situations when we interact with them (and often through a third party). It can come as a surprise to learn how well someone 'knows' us when we are given the opportunity to receive open and honest feedback. Yet we should not be surprised; they are observing what we communicate to them through the words and behaviours we use.

Although we may not be aware of much change in our behaviour over time reality tends to be something quite different when we receive feedback. This is when learning to be aware is recognized as a valuable part of the enabler's toolkit. Awareness helps us be sensitive to the different ways we deal with people, how it affects them and how it changes over time. If you think about someone you know well, you could probably list several ways in which that person has changed over the past five to ten years. Now apply the same process to yourself and identify how you have changed. An enabler develops a level of awareness which detects the subtle changes and how these affect others.

It is important to understand how we express ourselves in the way we talk and the emphasis we add to certain parts of the communication. We also communicate by the way we look, the expressions we project, the way we stand and our general posture, i.e. by our body language. Because many of us have been conditioned by what we have heard, seen or believe we project this into our perception of people. Conditioning can be extremely powerful, enough to contaminate a person's senses which could produce a different 'reality' from the one which really exists.

Enablers avoid judging a person against pre-conceived notions which result in a self-fulfilling prophecy. Awareness encourages an open-minded approach to how others project themselves by what they say and the body language used. As time passes the enabler develops a sense of what each person is attempting to achieve in the relationship and how they express themselves in their own way. Enablers themselves strive to ensure that thoughts expressed are supported by appropriate body language which communicates congruence to others. Achieving congruence in what we say, do and mean enables us to build trust into our relationships. The more others trust us, the greater their willingness will be to share their perceptions of how we affect them and others.

Travelling light

Confidence is built on a foundation of increasing self-awareness which enables us to examine how we affect and influence other people. Through feedback and disclosure we are able to examine how our thinking and actions are perceived by others. When we discover that some of our values and beliefs are not consistent with where we believe we are in our development, we can modify them. This is a process for which we have coined the term 'discharging our historical baggage'.

This concept depicts people walking around with enormous suitcases full of experiences which are no longer relevant to the lives they lead today. Many of us live in the past and it can come as quite a surprise to learn how much this influences our ability to handle situations today and in the future. We need to examine these experiences and to retain those which are relevant whilst discarding the baggage which has no real relevance to the life we lead at present. We need to recognize the speed of change and the uncertainty that it brings. The more we are able to detach ourselves from the past the better able we shall be to face the realities of today.

Regular international travellers have long recognized the value of 'travelling light'. They ensure they have just enough with them to meet their business and personal needs. This is achieved through careful thought and planning based on previous experiences updated to take account of future needs. An important part of developing self-awareness then involves us in examining our thinking to identify historical components which positively influence our values, beliefs and attitudes, and through which our behaviour is displayed. As we face the challenges of today, we begin to understand the importance congruence plays in our transactions with others.

Influence of culture

When developing self-awareness we should also be aware of the influence culture has on our attitudes, growth and development. In western cultures the accent would be on the individual as independent, competitive and self-contained. In other cultures the individual would be an integral part of a more homogeneous society. Allowing for the different influences of culture there is still a growing acceptance of the proposition that we must understand ourselves before we can understand others. The proposition makes sense in a wide variety of situations as the more equipped we are to understand what is happening, the more appropriate our response will be. The key to being an enabler depends on a very highly developed self-awareness which provides sensitive antennae to sense what is happening around us as we interact with people from our own and different cultures.

For example, organizations all over the world are faced with the need to discover ways to maintain their competitive edge. This involves developing strategies which enable the organization to re-position itself in changing markets. The most vital strategy involves the personnel of the business. We hear a great deal about participative management being the next solution to our problems. From our perspective this involves developing a participative process whereby all the people are involved in achieving the organizational goals by being committed to contributing to their fulfilment in an effective manner.

Participative management creates an environment which encourages all employees to be involved and committed to shared objectives. To many managers this sounds like a concept which would fit, or already fits, their current organization. Yet when we observe the way some of these managers talk about their employees and how they behave when dealing with them, we find a serious lack of congruence. This is called the 'knowing/doing syndrome' which implies that although a person may understand the situation, intellectually their behaviour and actions say something quite different. Awareness of the need to translate our thinking into appropriate action is an important part of the enabling process. Developing our awareness to enable us to remove or reduce the possibility of operating under only the knowing part of the knowing/doing syndrome, is therefore a prerequisite.

AWARENESS OF OTHERS

Understanding ourselves is the first step in developing an awareness of how to relate to other people in an effective and positive manner. One of the significant components of the future we believe will be cooperation based on respect for individuals coupled with an environment which encourages them to make an effective contribution to society. People will learn to relate to each other as a positive process which can produce solutions to individual and collective opportunities and problems. Against this backcloth we have to use our awareness of how others 'tick' to enable us achieve effective relationships.

What we are portraying is not an idyllic picture of people living in some sunny Utopia. In our view, an effective relationship implies the desire to relate to others, with a willingness to work together, to produce results. People will not be required to like each other or be involved in social intercourse if they do not wish to be. However, it certainly does mean individuals respecting each other and valuing all races and creeds.

Historical awareness

Many countries now have multiracial societies. This creates tension as each ethnic group strives to find a niche in the new land. Conditioning from the media and education has tended to leave a minority of the indigenous population with views which make them hostile to the new citizens. An enabler will be very aware of the values and beliefs which have been inculcated over the years. These will at times come into focus and shape our attitudes and behaviour. However much the picture was 'true' in the past, we shall be aware of how people change.

Part of the enabler's responsibility is to understand how to help people of different ethnic origins adapt to their new society. The process will take many generations as all parties learn tolerance in accepting the others' wishes and traditions. There is a natural desire for people to want to keep alive the heritage and traditions of their native land; just as it is natural for indigenous citizens to feel resentment when foreign citizens do not respect their traditions and heritage by wishing to live in their own cultural groups. Recognizing that most of these desires are natural and with respect for each other's views and customs, a new order will emerge which reflects compassion, understanding and acceptance of the needs of people in a rapidly changing world.

The challenge we face in the future lies in our desire and ability to understand each other in a manner which acknowledges our similarities and differences. In most instances when people are willing to work together to reach an understanding in an environment of mutual respect, differing values are listened to and accepted. Then the will exists to find a solution which allows us to move forward with a sense of consensus. If there is a real willingness to explore issues to find win/win solutions, they will be found irrespective of how many differences exist beforehand. Within this framework of cooperation lies our future potential to develop socieites which meet the needs of multi-racial groups and provide fulfilment. Progress to this end will come from our recognition of the importance of relating to and understanding other people. What may emerge from this process is a new order which incorporates the best practices from each of the different cultures to shape the 'new' culture.

Trust in relationships

The ability to develop, maintain and end relationships in a productive and positive manner will be in demand as we move into the future. In addition, good relationships can provide us with feedback opportunities which are essential in enabling us to continue to develop our awareness. Understanding the many benefits to be derived from effective relationships should motivate us to work hard at acquiring a high level of self-awareness.

Trust is a fundamental element in all effective relationships. Therefore, if we have as one of our objectives the building of relationships based on trust, we are in tune with the aim of an enabler. This is one of the main reasons we need to develop a high level of awareness. As we journey through life we have many opportunities to learn about the effect we have on each relationship. Each situation can provide clues to help us understand the impact our behaviour has on those involved. We have a responsibility to be able to read the clues and thus gain valuable understanding from the insights.

From these insights we learn that people are different and as such have different needs. Increasing our awareness, therefore, enables us to tune into and understand the different needs of different people. From this process we can acquire information and understanding on how we need to behave to meet the trust-building needs of others. In addition, we need to be aware that our behaviour will be observed by others who may not be in direct contact with us. We should, therefore, work at building trust in a way which communicates our aims to all whoever and wherever they may be.

Managing relationships

Trust, as the fundamental ingredient in a relationship, will be developed in different ways to meet the needs of each individual. It may be useful to explore what the outcome may be when there is trust in a relationship. Such a relationship will enable the participants to handle all types of situation in a positive manner. Information received by each person will be used as a basis for achieving understanding. Issues which may have a negative or potentially hostile content will be confronted positively with a desire to seek a win/win solution. If in the last resort the issue involves a fundamental challenge to values, the relationship would be closed with care and understanding being expressed by both parties. And, if this happened, each person would not expect the other to denigrate the relationship at a later date. In fact there would remain the potential framework for the relationship to be renewed if circumstances changed for one or other of the parties.

The main question is 'how do we learn to build trust in relationships?' The answer is in our belief in ourselves and respect for others and how this is displayed in the behaviours we use in relationships. If we really want to build trust we behave in a consistent manner designed to project empathy. When empathy exists in a relationship, we accept the other person, for whatever he or she may be, and are willing to communicate with them in an honest way. It also means that we do what we say we shall do and avoid the danger of being less than genuine in our transactions. Most of us know intuitively if we are being dealt with in a way which lacks legitimacy. We can often detect when promises will not be kept or when confidences will not be respected.

Relationships, therefore, provide us with the opportunity to be truly empathetic and through our empathy be open, honest, accepting of others, consistent and reliable. In fact, all our behaviour and actions will communicate to others a consistent level of congruence.

Building our awareness provides us with the skills to build bridges to enable effective relationships to be established. The bridges will be of as many varieties as there are people but they will contain the essential ingredients of respect for others, empathy, trust and a genuine desire to understand. When individuals construct barriers through historical or biased thinking, enablers will seek creative solutions which produce win/win outcomes. Enablers will encourage people to avoid being trapped by thinking which is biased prejudiced and fearful. They will help us see beyond the current issue and explore options which can provide different solutions.

ENVIRONMENTAL AWARENESS

As our confidence grows through developing awareness we can learn to be more aware of what is occurring in the variety of situations in which we are involved. If we extend our awareness to the business world, we call the situations 'environments' to describe sets of characteristics which facilitate people to achieve organizational goals. Being able to identify, interpret and understand each environment helps us assess where and when an intervention would be appropriate to improve the process.

Describing an organization

When describing an organization we think about it in the widest sense to include family, school, social group, sports club and any other group which meets for a purpose. When we are about to be involved in any of these organizations we should naturally be interested in understanding the environment within which it operates. We are then aware of the people and circumstances which influence the environment. Understanding its purpose should enable us to see the direction it is taking and whether this fits with our personal value systems. The better the fit, the more likely we shall be to be committed to making an effective contribution.

We tend to feel better about being involved in an organization which has a clear direction and purpose because then we can see the contribution we can make to it. If an organization has a sharp focus on its direction and involes us in the process of developing this focus, it will gain a higher level of commitment from us and from our increased commitment will flow the energy and drive to help it achieve its goals.

Recognizing the value which clarity of direction gives an organization should motivate us to develop the awareness and skills which would enable us to analyse what exists in any environment. It can be very frustrating to be involved in an activity in a new environment in which we feel ill at ease. Our unease could be due to not understanding the procedures and customs or in not knowing when to make our contribution. Being aware of what is going on and how we can play our part makes us feel good. This can act as a powerful motivator to encourage us to extend our awareness and be able to understand what different environments have to offer.

Exploring an environment

There are a number of general rules regarding the structure of an environment which can help us build a framework of understanding. These can be briefly stated as follows:

- identify who is the host, chair or organizer of the event
- seek to find the purpose and expected outcomes of the event
- discover why you have been invited and what your expected role is
- find out who else is involved and if they represent a number of different groups
- attempt to find out if there are any customs or precepts to which you will be expected to conform
- identify the timeframe and other logistics
- assess what involvement, if any, is expected after the event
- find out if the event has been sponsored.

Our aim should be to explore the environment to identify the factors which could affect our involvement and performance. Understanding who the principal players are and what they expect to achieve can provide a basis on which we can start to understand our role in the scenario. As we identify each factor, we can begin to build a clearer picture of the environment. As the picture takes shape we can determine what is expected of us and ensure we are adequately prepared.

Test assumptions

Awareness of the environment gives us the opportunity to chart a path which enables us to make an effective contribution if and when required. We feel confident at all times as we use our skills to assess events as they occur to test our earlier assumptions. Identifying the factors from which we can assess potential strategies enables us to be prepared for an increasing range of eventualities. If we have the confidence to make assumptions about the environment we have a strategy to suit plus a process to test these assumptions as we are involved in the event.

The key to raising our awareness comes from developing a curiosity, coupled with a desire, to understand situations. We are not prepared to accept situations at face value as we believe that there are a number of factors at play even in the most simple situations. Our curiosity leads us to attempt to identify and analyse the factors. This can provide insights which equip us with awareness and understanding of what we can contribute to the situation. In the process we shall be looking for clues which help us understand the environment.

Moving from the general, let us explore what we can do to raise our awareness in business environments. The first priority is to understand the purpose and objectives of the organization to enable us understand what our contribution can be. To help us understand the purpose and objectives, we shall need to learn to undertake three specific and integrated steps as follows:

- scan the environment
- identify signposts
- understand strategic directions.

Scanning the environment

Being able to understand and explore the different environments in which the organization exists, or relates to, is a vital part of the awareness building process. Scanning different environments involves defining each one and developing criteria which can be used to test the present and compare the future.

Once we have established the criteria which enable us to understand clearly where we are currently placed, we are in a better position to anticipate the future. Technology can now help in this forward-looking process through modelling techniques using a computer. The computer has the facility to input a number of variables and to process them so as to produce different scenarios. The interesting part of the process is in discovering the effect each change has on the previous scenario. A computer really comes into its own with the speed by which it can process the information.

If we do not have access to a computer this should not prevent us from attempting to scan and understand environment manually. We can still gather information which will be invaluable in determining future strategic directions. As we scan each environment and build our knowledge base and understanding of the implications we should have a better sense of the impact of potential change. Recognizing we exist in dynamic environments, and that we ourselves are involved in a process of change, enables us to understand that others are in exactly the same position. The enabler's task is to encourage people in an organization to move from a reactive to a proactive mode, thus changing from looking backwards to looking forwards and shaping strategies and managing resources to achieve desired results.

As we scan different environments we collect data on a wide range of issues within the context of a political, social, economic, enironmental and psychological framework. Our task will be to identify and record each indicator with a view to determining what it means to our organization. We need to develop our awareness in two distinct areas. Firstly, to identify the signposts which indicate the strategic directions our organization is following. And secondly, to identify and interpret the signposts picked up from our environmental scanning. These can help in shaping organizational strategic directions to meet future perceived needs/opportunities.

Strategic signposts

We need to search for the 'signposts' which signal current and future potential direction. These signposts will generally make a statement about a perceived trend, or desired outcome, the organization needs to be aware of. The following are examples of strategic signposts:

- to maintain profitability we need to expand market share of product '*x*' by 25 per cent over the next three years
- acid rain is destroying our lakes and forests
- youth unemployment represents a large sector of depreciating human assets – opportunities must be created for them
- we need to buy a house with extra rooms to accommodate the expected increase in our family
- we shall create opportunities for female staff to be promoted to more senior levels
- we have lost 25 per cent of our skilled labour mainly due to emigration to Australia over the past two years
- quality must be our No. 1 concern if we are to maintain our market position
- we need to develop ways of involving our staff in decision making.

Each signpost offers an insight into issues the organization may need to address if it wishes to remain effective. By identifying and stating clearly each relative signpost the organization should be able to build up a picture of its future potential position. From this strategic directions will emerge which the organization may decide to follow. Identifying strategic signposts provides an opportunity to help shape the organization's future strategy. It adds value to the internal self-diagnosis of current organization directions by providing inputs and benchmarks to test current assumptions on which strategy has been constructed.

Confronting assumptions

Challenging assumptions is an important part of the enabler's role as it plays a vital role in the process of obtaining clarity of vision of the future. It involves recognizing that most people are more comfortable with the present because, even if it is unpalatable, 'the certainty of today's misery is better than the misery of tomorrow's uncertainy.' This sort of thinking acts as a brake on change and is often associated with the 'yes . . . but' syndrome. In this instance it is 'yes . . . but we can't because we tried that before and it did not work.' You will probably be able to relate to this and many similar statements which are used to block discussion and examination of issues which may have the potential to produce effective results.

There is a strong tendency in many organizational cultures to accept as 'fact' information which is largely based on assumptions. Many statements are proffered in a manner designed to inhibit discussion and examination. They often reflect genuinely-held views based on experience which is given to avoid 'reinventing the wheel'. These unquestioned assertions, although possibly valid in the past, need to be examined again to test their relevance to today.

The enabler will therefore encourage people to look to the future to confront and challenge any statements or behaviour designed to block examination of solutions. This challenging will be done in a way which enables individuals making blocking statements to express the circumstances around the particular issue. Encouraging them to express the facts on which they base such statements should offer the opportunity to put the issues clearly out in the open. It is surprising how few of the blocking statements can subsequently stand this process of positive examination. This is because many people are unaware of the passage of time and the changing circumstances between past incidents and today. By using a positive process which enables the issues to surface, the awareness can provide a basis for moving from stating difficulties to solution-seeking. Once in this solution-seeking mode, we can develop scenarios for future strategic directions.

Our thrust has been to raise our awareness to identify the signposts which indicate trends which could be important to our organization. We then need to develop our ability to interpret the signs and make sense of what they indicate and how this may affect our organization. Some signposts will flag major implications which significantly influence future strategic directions. This points to the added value benefits derived from the process.

Strategic directions

An effective organization will have produced a checklist of what it aims to achieve from the use of its resources. The direction will be communicted to all its people in such a way that it provides them with a purpose and direction. They will feel involved and committed to making their contribution to achieve the corporate goals through which their personal goals will be fulfilled.

Understanding the relevant environments establishes a foundation on which the organization can determine strategic directions. Each strategic direction provides a clear statement to all. This statement may say where the organization is heading and what it will do to get there. To illustrate the point, the following examples are drawn from current strategic plans:

- we shall cease manufacture of product 'y' in two years' time
- our thrust will be to become less dependent on skilled labour by implementing a policy of contract labour
- all head office support functions will be decentralized to the branches within eighteen months
- rewards will be based on a performance-related process by the end of the next financial year.

Strategic directions would be woven together to form an integrated strategic plan. Our awareness enables us continually to test if what we perceive in the environment is congruent with the organization's strategic plan. Enablers develop the capacity to see the overall picture and thus use their skills to focus on the small parts which need to be examined. The effect is one of seeing what is happening on many different levels whilst monitoring a sense of reality about where the organization is currently positioned. People are encouraged to be outward looking with the aim of being able to understand when change should be implemented to maintain business effectiveness.

In most instances an organization will have more than one strategic direction to achieve its mission. The greater awareness the organization has, the more likely it will sense and detect opportunities. Its people will also tend to be sensitive to and aware of the implications of being flexible in their approach to achieving the organization's outputs.

It should be clear by now that we are talking about a process which encourages regular involvement to maintain its relevance. Once an organization has developed future scenarios and described its stretegic directions, it will also develop a process of reviewing them on a regular basis. Enablers believe that reviewing involves an acceptance of the validity of the statements within a framework of recognition that time can change the relativity and relevance of the factors involved. Therefore in a period of rapid change we may find that reviewing should be done on a continuous basis by selecting different aspects to be examined during a particular period of each year.

USING AWARENESS

Being aware gives us the opportunity to be a positive asset to others. We are able to 'sense' the needs of others and determine the appropriate behaviour to meet them. In addition, we are in a sound position to assist our organization obtain clarity on its direction through identifying strategic signposts.

Awareness helps us facilitate change as we are sensitive to each situation through our diagnosis of the various environments. This provides us with insights into what might need to be modified to enable a new and more effective organization to be realized. Being able to play a positive part in enabling people and organizations to position themselves to achieve desired results is the task of an enabling leader.

Awareness is a multifaceted range of skills which enable us to relate to people and environments in an effective manner. We aim to create or influence environments to establish climates which foster the release of individual talent in a constructive manner. Awareness assists us to obtain clarity about where we are aiming and how we can get there. It offers us a results orientation based on achievement through the contribution made by all. We shall operate in a genuine and authentic manner which encourages the appropriate balance between individual and team contribution.

Enabling leadership will empower due to the way enablers relate to others. Awareness is the core of enabling as it provides the foundation on which an enabler's personal philosophy is constructed (see Chapter 5).

CONCEPTS EXPLORED IN CHAPTER 5

BELIEF IN, AND RESPECT FOR, SELF AND OTHERS
  Avoid Judging People
  Meeting Needs
  Self-Responsibility
BUILD GENUINE RELATIONSHIPS
  Openness and Trust
  Reliability
  Trust-building Never Stops
  Sharing and Caring
  Adversarial/Collaborative Relationships
  Self-leadership
SEEK WIN/WIN SOLUTIONS
  Generic Negotiating Strategies
AIM TO EMPOWER
  Competent and Aware
  Learning from Experience
  Empowering Others
VISION OF THE FUTURE
  Forward-looking
  Learn from Experience
  Sense of Movement
  Able to Envision
  Shape the Future
ACHIEVEMENT ORIENTATION
  Commitment

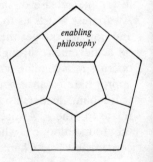

enabling philosophy

5 Enabling philosophy

The *Oxford Dictionary* defines 'enable' as 'to make able, to give power, strength or authority to, to make possible'. The definition provides a useful base for exploring and understanding what makes a person an enabler. It centres on the concept of 'to give power and make possible'. We are constantly reminded of the difference in outcome from an activity which is enabled, compared with ones which are not.

Close examination of the data leads us to the realization that the major difference is in how an enabler relates to others. In most cases they are thought of as able and credible people who have an added asset in the way they create an effective learning environment. Time and again, enablers are described as 'being able to draw the best from individuals by the way they act and react within a positive environment'.

Enablers are people who have a personal philosophy by which they live their lives and relate to others. From our research we conclude that an enabler is a person who believes in empowering which can be described as:

- multi-purpose as it concerns us, as an individual, and in what we do with our lives and in our relationships with others
- encouragement to find opportunities to create and maintain a climate within which we and others can grow.

As we learn more about enablers a set of common personal values emerges. Although in many instances the words used to describe the values are different, the outcome from their use is consistent. We observe a high level of congruence in their application and this gives us the confidence to share them with you. The core personal values which are shared by a significant number of enablers are:

- belief in and respect for self and others
- build genuine relationships
- seek win/win solutions
- aim to empower
- vision of the future
- achievement orientation.

It is fascinating to observe how many of the enablers share these values and use them to guide their lives. Although there is consistency in the values used, each person has acquired a personal philosophy and a unique way. As the ideas develop, it is apparent that each of us can use our own experiences to help construct an enabling philosophy by examining each value and comparing it with our present values and beliefs. This will enable us to determine what action, if any, we need to take to modify our 'mind sets' and be able to behave more as an enabling leader.

If we aim to be enablers, the journey we take does not require us to follow the one and only route. As we learn to be more creative in our learning we discover that there are many paths we can take to acquire, develop and live by an enabling philosophy.

Each value is explored in more depth to provide a basis of understanding with the caveat that we do not see them as discrete entities. They are all interdependent and when woven together form each person's unique enabling philosophy.

BELIEF IN, AND RESPECT FOR, SELF AND OTHERS

This is at the core of the enabler's philosophy. Enablers have a strong belief in themselves which is developed on real awareness of the need to be open and sensitive to what is happening in each environment in which they find themselves. To obtain an accurate understanding of the environments they have developed antennae to enable them to sense, and test the reality of each situation. As their ability to sense and interpret develops, they become more assured in determining what action to take and when.

With awareness enablers can test the reality of situations as they identify and interpret the key factors. One of the fundamentals is to look for what has stimulated the person to behave in a particular positive (or negative) manner. Enablers will understand that people tend to react to forces within themselves triggered by intrinsic or extrinsic stimuli. They avoid being 'hooked' on what a person has done; instead they focus on the cause which generally throws a different light on the matter. At the heart of this process of attempting to understand why an individual acts and behaves in a particular way is the enablers' inherent belief in people. They understand that most individuals are basically positive.

Avoid judging people

The enabler's belief and respect encompasses the total spectrum of known human behaviour however it is expresed. Experience teaches them that people are influenced by the behaviour of others and that this affects their own behaviour. If they are met with positive behaviour they are inclined to feel good and respond likewise. Alternatively, they are just as likely to react negatively in situations where they are exposed to negative and deviant behaviour from others. Enablers avoid allowing their thinking to be clouded by these different behaviours. They believe in the potential for positiveness by the majority and respect what an individual projects as an expression in response to perceived/felt needs. However different the behaviours are, enablers will respect an individual's position without judging whether it is right or wrong. They believe that it is vital to be able to distance themselves from any tendency to jump to conclusions or become emotionally involved.

Meeting needs

As confidence grows, enablers are able to communicate with increasing effectiveness. Their aim is to achieve a high level of understanding with others by being competent and caring. As they learn to understand how their thinking and actions affect others, they can differentiate those actions which enhance relationships from those which sour them. Feedback gives enablers an awareness of how others perceive them and how appropriate their behaviour is in meeting others' needs. In addition, the more effective enablers become in identifying the needs of others, the better positioned they are to behave appropriately to meet individual needs. This in turn enables individuals to meet the enabler's needs.

Understanding the effect they have on others, coupled with the ability to modify behaviour to meet others' needs, endows enablers with a growing self-assurance as their skills and relationships flourish. From this strength a growing conviction emerges of the potential to create effective and productive relationships. From improving relationships they develop a respect for all people with everyone being treated consistently.

Self-responsibility

Throughout all stages of interactions, and when involved in individual activities, enablers will apply a strong code of self-responsibility. Acting in a manner which destroys trust or creates false hopes is avoided as enablers can see the dangers of action designed to gain short-term results, particularly when a longer-term focus is required. They will strive for clarity and understanding of what needs to be done by themselves or in offering help to others with awareness of the powerful benefits derived from trusting relationships which empower others to develop in their own way. Building up the range of relationships which offer positive outcomes is achieved by being consistent in the application of the enabler's belief in, and respect for, others.

BUILD GENUINE RELATIONSHIPS

This aspect of an enabling leader's philosophy is fundamental to achieving results in all areas of life. Each relationship is treated with respect and therefore founded on genuine motives. Relating to others in a genuine way is crucial to effectiveness. The main elements involved in developing and maintaining genuine relationships are:

- Openness and trust
- Reliability
- Risk taking
- Sharing and caring.

Let us now discuss how each of the elements plays its part in securing genuine relationships.

Openness and trust

An essential part of developing quality relationships is building them on a foundation of trust. Trust is one element of a relationship which we know exists or not. It is often thought to be intangible and to defy description; that is, until we look at the behaviours we use to relate to others.

When a relationship is based on trust both parties act responsibly in their transactions. Their aim is to generate solutions to enable them to achieve their goals. Through their openness they are able to handle all issues by being receptive, listening to each others' views and working at finding a solution. If the views and aims are too diverse they will agree to differ, leave the issue then move on to the next one. They will remain open to ideas which may resolve the problem/opportunity and will be free to approach it from other angles. Purpose and direction are achieved as both parties 'walk and talk' with a genuine desire to achieve a positive outcome.

Enablers project a high degree of openness through the use of disclosure and feedback. Openness can be assessed by how much is disclosed about a particular issue or individual; how feedback is given; and the degree to which the individual is personally involved. Enablers believe that being genuine with others, in a way which does not disable them, provides a sound base on which openness can be constructed.

Enablers have a desire for relationships built on trust as it allows them to be open and responsive. They also believe productivity and creativity flourish in an environment where trust exists. Issues of all types can be handled in an open and sensitive manner when the objective of those involved is to reach mutually satisfactory solutions. Negative behaviour associated with people being defensive about change, usually in a low-trust environment, can be replaced by constructive attitudes. This encourages enablers to take risks in their interpersonal transactions with the aim of resolving conflict through positive confrontation. Individuals are often able to handle 'bad' news from a person they trust as they know it is honestly given and not designed to hurt them. Openness is one of the essentials of trust as it enables a sound basis for the relationship to be constructed.

Reliability

As individuals learn to trust enablers through the consistent way they interact with them, they begin to learn the importance of reliability in relationships. In our view reliability is a major characteristic of an enabling leader. Being able to fulfil what was agreed is important in all relationships. This challenges the tendency to agree to do something without really accepting full responsibility for its delivery. Enabling involves understanding the significance of reliability in relationships and if we make an offer to undertake some task, it will be fulfilled. If we behave like this, that is what people will come to accept and respect. Through our reliability, consistency and competence we create a framework on which trust will be constructed.

Trust-building never stops

It is also vital for us to understand that trust-building never stops. We don't just gain trust and then stop; it is a process which needs our constant attention. The way we interact is being assessed in terms of the degree of openness, consistency, reliability and genuineness we project. As we develop, over time, a pattern of positive behaviour to which individuals can relate and be comfortable we gain their trust.

When involved in a genuine relationship we find that it has the characteristics of openness and trust. All issues are raised and confronted in a positive manner with the purpose of being resolved to each party's benefit. There can be lightness in the relationship which frees those involved to attempt creative solutions, and when relationships come to an end the process is managed in a manner which leaves the parties feeling all right.

The soundness of such relationships can set a climate of risk-taking resulting in the generation of higher-level solutions. When we feel it is safe to be adventurous in this environment we can produce creative ideas. Being able to 'let go' of our historical baggage and project our thinking in a forward direction is a desired outcome of genuine relationships, with the results of our efforts being assessed by the creative solutions we generate.

Sharing and caring

We discovered that enablers live by the motto 'the more you give, the more you receive'. This view of giving is not prompted by a belief that it will secure expected returns. It stems from an objective reality that the more they give from a sharing/caring desire, the more they receive because others recognize the legitimacy of their contributions. Once again, the genuineness of the motive plays a significant part in establishing trust which encourages individuals to respond positively.

Most of us want to make a contribution when we understand the goals to aim for, and feel involved in determining how they can be accomplished. This allows us to make use of our knowledge and skills with an attitude of achievement. Our involvement enables us to discover the mix of knowledge and skills required to achieve. In addition we operate within a climate of cooperation which can encourage us to improve our performance. Thus we find that our knowledge, skills and attitude are blended into a cohesive force by the environment, which encourages and rewards such behaviour.

Given the opportunity to be involved in creating a purposeful, caring and fulfilling environment, individuals naturally feel committed to its success. And they also feel good about sharing the benefits based on the contribution each member makes. Enablers demonstrate this care for those who are unable to make a contribution because of age, ability, handicap or for some other reason. Instead of ignoring or judging them, they are motivated to help them feel part of the community and thus retain their self-respect.

Enablers will work at helping individuals discover what they feel they can contribute with the belief that they have something to give. They will be encouraged to play their part within a nurturing environment which acknowledges their contribution however great or small. This expression of belief in sharing can make all our lives full and enjoyable because it gives meaning and purpose.

Adversarial/collaborative relationships

We believe that the key to quality, productivity and effectiveness is the ability to create genuine relationships which is in direct conflict with the general trend in many parts of society. For example, the adversarial climate of much of the current business, political and social scene creates an environment of distrust, anger, closed minds and energy being converted into game playing or 'politics'. The enabler's objective is to replace these with cooperative attitudes and thus construct collaborative cultures.

Developing values to support a collaborative culture would bring sharply into focus the inappropriate nature of much of today's business language. Superior/subordinate, leader/follower, manager/worker and control/discipline are terms which reinforce the concept of master/slave relationships. Enablers understand that people are different, bring different skills, knowledge and attitudes, and make different levels of contribution. However, if they enable individuals to relate in a truly collaborative culture they would release their potential in a synergistic manner. We no longer need to construct hierarchical and authoritarian regimes when we understand and believe that people can be responsible when given a real opportunity.

Self-leadership

As enablers work at building genuine relationships the idea of superior and subordinate becomes an increasingly outdated concept. It reinforces ineffective traditional organizational practices. Genuine relationships encourage individuals to be self-directed leaders as there are many reasons to support the practice of everyone being a leader. If we feel able and confident to be a leader, the probability is high that we shall act as a leader. Our leadership would be within the context of equality in that we would be encouraged to act as leader when we have the appropriate skills and knowledge. If we did not have the skills or knowledge, enablers would encourage us to operate as leaders, thus giving us the freedom to succeed or fail. Individuals would not feel subservient as they would be aware of the opportunities for them to be leaders. In effect there are many occasions where multi-level leadership is required. When we have a clear goal orientation and an understanding of task interdependence we will find many opportunities to practise enabling leadership.

SEEK WIN/WIN SOLUTIONS

Individuals mean a great deal to enablers and this induces personal behaviour which shows consistent respect for everyone. Therefore, opportunities are found to create win/win solutions to all interpersonal situations. Solutions are sought based on finding out what are the real needs of those involved. This means being genuinely interested in others. To achieve effective results we need to exhibit a high level of empathy in our interactions with individuals. This requires us to relate to their feelings in a way which enables them to feel good. Relationships are developed from this base of understanding which allows us to transact a solution designed to be win/win.

When offered the privilege of hearing about a person's problems or opportunities enablers are afforded a rare chance to build trust. By active listening they gain the confidence of others and encourage them to feel free to disclose. This means suppressing a natural desire to interrupt and offer suggestions on what they think is wrong or what should be done to put it right. Instead enablers encourage individuals to explore the issue and obtain clarity through a process of sensitive and open-ended questioning. The purpose is to clarify the issue to obtain understanding on what the real factors are. Using a creative thinking process, enablers can discover ideas which give the individual the opportunity to achieve a win/win result. The process will make demands on all to be flexible in handling each transaction to ensure that the solutions are 'owned' by the person.

The enabler's motivation is in a belief that there are win/win solutions to be found which all will consider fair. Being positive in outlook and working to create a climate which encourages people to work together, enables individuals to search for and find mutually acceptable solutions. The key is to seek processes which enable them to work together to achieve their goals without disabling other people.

Awareness of the prevailing adversarial culture in many countries is important in understanding why people are influenced to expect negotiations to be win/lose. The challenge enablers face is therefore significant and gives them ample opportunity for creative solution-seeking. Being congruent in their actions with the aim of developing trust in all relationships, enablers can eventually encourage individuals to take personal risks and look for win/win solutions.

Generic negotiating strategies

Enablers also encourage individuals to think about the attitudes they hold before and during a transaction or negotiation. It comes as a surprise to some when they realize that they have entered a transaction with a losing attitude without really being aware of the fact. Exploring the four generic negotiating strategies can give useful insights on the strategy we have been using.

Figure 5.1 indicates the behaviours which tend to be used in each of the strategies. **Concessions** are made to keep people happy and show a willingness to move on the issue being transacted. It seldom succeeds as a strategy as others can perceive it as a weakness and thus expect other concessions to follow. When a person has a strong desire to achieve a result which fits his/her goals irrespective of the needs of others, they have a tendency to use **coercion**. Power or powerlessness is at the base of coercion and the outcome is always negative with one party feeling they have lost.

lose/win *concession*	*win/win* *consensus*
lose/lose *compromise*	*win/lose* *coercion*

Figure 5.1   Generic negotiating strategies

Compromise is a strategy which is used extensively to resolve many interpersonal transactions. In its best and most positive sense it means going more than half way to meet the other person's needs. However, in the 'normal' sense it means a little bit of coercion and concession dependent on the ebb and flow of power. In the 'normal' mode, outcomes tend to be more negative with all parties feeling less than satisfied with the result: hence the lose/lose position. If operated in the positive mode the process is closer to consensus which involves a genuine desire to understand the other person's needs.

Enablers have developed the ability to operate in a **consensus** mode as befits their belief in and respect for self and others. They understand that little will be achieved in a transaction until the other person's needs are understood. Once this has been achieved, the process of reaching a win/win can take place with each individual being involved in give and take based on a 'what if' approach. The outcome will generally be one which leaves all parties satisfied, not only at the conclusion, but also after the event.

By working with people to reach win/win solutions, enablers develop the awareness of the power of consensus and how it can achieve productive outputs. As individuals learn to trust the process and are willing to invest the time to make it work effectively, they will be less inclined to regress to other strategies to achieve results. Their awareness of the benefits far outstripping the time investment will be high. In addition, the positive relationship which emerges from the process provides sound evidence of how effective a win/win environment is for interpersonal transactions.

AIM TO EMPOWER

Empowering is the main driving force of the enabler. It is displayed in two distinct yet integrated parts: enablers have a mission to use every opportunity life provides to develop themselves, and through self-empowering, to assist others in a responsible manner to be empowered.

Self-empowering is achieved through:

- a desire to develop own competence
- being aware
- being a life-long learner
- experiential processes
- relationships with others.

Enablers want to operate in an effective and competent manner which produces results. This drive is based on a belief that performance can be continuously improved. Therefore, enablers seek opportunities to acquire the knowledge, skills and techniques which help to improve performance. They recognize the need to make their contribution to whatever activity or relationship in which they are involved. The quality of the contribution thus provides a sound foundation which others will understand, appreciate and reward as appropriate. Being competent is a state enablers strive to achieve as a means of playing their part in achieving their goals.

Competent and aware

Developing competence will be enhanced by being aware of the need for improvement coupled with a desire to acquire the necessary skills. It comes through a drive for understanding how and when to make their contribution. The outputs will be the building of confidence as each assignment is effectively accomplished. Self-empowering encourages enablers to be open and prepared for change. New situations will be explored for the opportunities they offer, rather than being viewed with uncertainty. Their positive attitude to change enables them to create an environment within which they approach the acquisition of knowledge and skill with positive anticipation.

Their interest and excitement in being competent thrives with their ready openness to explore options. Looking for learning opportunities is second nature to them and is accepted as a process available during their lifespan. Each learning opportunity is explored to determine what benefits can be obtained which will improve performance. As they progress through each learning experience their awareness helps them shape the opportunity to meet specific needs. They test their understanding of what is being achieved by applying learning in different situations to observe its effects. Drawing the best out of each experience allows enablers to continue to develop and improve.

Learning from experience

Observing enablers in the self-empowering process is enlightening as their motivation to learn is linked to developing self-confidence. There appears to be a high degree of singlemindedness coupled with an appreciation of others in the process. Awareness tells the enabler that improving competence is very much dependent on the positive assistance given by others. Enablers depend to varying degrees on learning from others which makes it vital to relate positively to people. This exemplifies the enablers' projection of sharing and caring through which people relate to them in a way which encourages them to continue their development. This ready giving by others is a welcome contribution to the enabler's growth and is accepted as a two-way process.

As enablers continue with the self-empowering process they seek opportunities to empower others. The mission of empowering involves them in a series of relationships. Enablers have an intrinsic desire to help people in a variety of ways which is accomplished through the manner by which they interact. Their respect for people and belief in their potential drives enablers to deal with each individual as an equal. They recognize the uniqueness of the individual and the need to treat each individual differently and with consistency. We stated earlier how central trust is to enabling relationships to be productive. It is through the development of this trust that empathy can be achieved.

Empowering others

We discovered that enablers practised empowering others as a part of their own self-empowering process. Their empowering mission is expressed as:

- a desire to help others (with no dependency)
- an awareness of others' needs
- a willingness to share/exchange
- fulfilment at seeing people grow and develop
- being at ease with people.

Reducing dependency

A main drive of the enabler is to help others by using a process which avoids the creation of a state of dependency. The enabler understands the natural tendency for people to become dependent on others. This is often reinforced by societal conditioning which encourages some people to think of themselves as being less able to look after themselves and thus need 'support'. Unfortunately we have observed professional help become a crutch on which individuals lean and become defensive and fearful if the help is withdrawn. Awareness of this powerful syndrome guides enablers to understand its effects on relationships.

In Chapter 10 we examine in detail attitudes to change and the reasons why individuals drift into dependent relationships. Taking time to explore and understand what individual expectations are and how these are translated into outputs can provide a sound basis on which help can be offered.

Understanding others

Understanding the needs of others is important if we are to be of real assistance. It involves enablers using an exploring and probing process to discover what is being expressed by an individual. Active listening and clarifying play a crucial role in the process of understanding. At times individuals may not have a clear picture of what they are seeking from a particular learning experience. At these points enablers avoid evaluation from their own experiences to 'tell' individuals what they should be doing. We discuss in Chapter 6 several different approaches which aid the process of assisting individuals obtain a sharp focus and understanding of their learning needs. For the moment we identify the danger of creating a learning environment which produces dependency.

Sharing

As part of their desire to empower, enablers accept the need to build relationships which provide an effective transfer of learning and competence. Their motivation is to share their knowledge, skills and experience as a means of providing others with the opportunity to compare with their own perceived reality. Sharing and exchanging of ideas, information and techniques is done with the purpose of enlarging the arenas of knowledge and understanding. Seeing people develop and grow in confidence resulting in increasing competence is sufficient reward in itself and gives the enabler a sense of fulfilment.

Expression of this element of enabling philosophy provides a framework which can encourage us to share for the collective benefit. Collaboration becomes an accepted part of life as we learn to relate to each other with increasing positiveness. It is an environment which draws the best from people as we feel that our contribution is appreciated. And we can gain mutual benefit in being both learners and enablers. Although people are different, the collaborative climate appears to create a framework which enables us to relate positively to each other with the probability that whatever task we undertake will be accomplished with success.

VISION OF THE FUTURE

Another of the main characteristics of enablers is their future orientation. When sharing with them, they have the ability to draw from a perspective of life which provides many interesting insights and realities. As issues are discussed, enablers recognize the value of thinking in a balanced and open manner which allows ideas to be explored from historical, present and future perspectives. Being able to develop ideas from a constantly shaping frame of reference allows the enabler to develop different scenarios for the future. Thus, breaking out of the self-imposed constraints of linear thinking fashions new thought patterns which encourage open-mindedness and a willingness to meet change positively.

When confronted with changing situations, enablers demonstrate their abilities by drawing on the following characteristics:

- being forward-looking
- learning from experience
- having a sense of movement
- able to envision
- ability to shape the future.

Forward-looking

It was interesting to observe how often enablers talked about what can be done in the future. They were continually exploring options which offered solutions to meet identified needs. They were easily distinguishable by the fact that their language spoke about the future and solutions, in contrast to others who appeared to talk about the past and tended to state difficulties. This is witnessed by the number of times a response is prefaced by 'yes . . . but . . .' which then contains all the reasons why the idea, comment, suggestion is not valid – that is, from the other person's mind set.

Enablers do not use the 'yes . . . but . . .' syndrome. Their aim is to explore opinions and encourage individuals to think beyond the boundaries. This can be illustrated by inviting you to try the nine-dot puzzle (Figure 5.2). Join the dots by drawing four straight lines which pass through all nine dots without lifting your pen from paper. You are allowed to cross through a straight line. If you are unaware of how to tackle the puzzle spend a few minutes thinking about a solution outside the nine dots. This piece of advice is used frequently in many organizations to encourage people to extend their thinking beyond their normal mind set.

One solution to the puzzle is shown at the end of the chapter (Figure 5.3) and illustrates how the answer lies outside the nine dot boundaries. Stretching their thinking to encompass new ideas based on facts and/or apparent fiction is a regular part of the enabler's way of life. By working at developing their thinking capacity and breaking loose occasionally from the constraints of

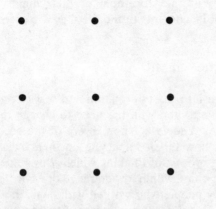

Figure 5.2   Nine dot puzzle (1)

linear thinking, enablers are able to enhance their capacity to use all parts of their mind. This allows them to be more open to change and new ideas and results in them having a future orientation.

Learn from experience

People with a future orientation tend to avoid investing a great deal of their energies conducting unnecessary post-mortems. They are aware of what was happening during an event and are able to determine the factors which contributed to its success or failure. Enablers have the capacity to be actively involved in assessing these factors as events unfold. Learning to capture the 'gems', the factors which contribute to the success or failure of an event, becomes second nature. They have become acutely aware of the negative power of historical baggage and how it can muddy the thinking process.

Being able to test realities on an ongoing basis is an effective way to understand what should be retained from experiential learning. Clearing our mind of experiences which have no real place in our lives today can be a valuable process by which to modify our historical frame of reference. When issues are raised which relate to the enabler's experience, these are tested in a constructive way by exploring the different views to see if a better solution can be discovered. Enablers recognize the need periodically to revisit the storeroom of their minds to reassess the relevance of its contents to the life they are currently living.

Sense of movement

As we move into the information and service age, many people are being confronted with the need to change the practices of a lifetime. Most people are now aware of the accelerating rate of change and how this is impacting on their lives. Enablers have developed a process of thinking which allows them to be open to what is happening within a wide range of environments. This was expressed by people who worked with enablers as their sense of movement. Enablers always appeared to be working with people on solutions which were designed to move the process forward.

In a business context, enablers were perceived to be people who did a great deal of walking and talking. They were seldom located in their office for lengthy periods unless involved with colleagues on actual issues. On most occasions they would be found walking around their area and in other areas listening to what people had to say and exchanging ideas on how progress could be achieved on a wide range of business and social issues.

These enablers believed that effective results were achieved by people at the sharp end of a business. They saw that everyone who could add value to the product or service was given the opportunity to do so. They worked at creating an environment which encouraged individuals to think about what they were doing and being responsible for the quality of their input. Being accepted as thinking people able to contribute to the improvement of their jobs and the organization's performance provides strong motivation for most. Enablers understand this and thus invest their time and energies creating environments which release such an outcome from those involved.

Able to envision

A part of shaping a positive environment comes from the enabler's ability to envision the various components and behaviours which are required to achieve effective results. Many individuals have a need to believe in the future and look for insights which help them obtain clarity and shape. It is here that enabling leadership plays a significant part. Enablers, being future-oriented and with a capacity to look for solutions outside the 'dots', can create visions of the future. Developing pictures or scenarios of the future provides options to which others can attempt to relate. By a process of sharing and exchanging ideas, the visionary can obtain greater clarity and, at the same time, others can understand better future possibilities.

An open-minded approach to life provides a social framework for exploring the future. Ideas and suggestions, however wild and unrealistic, can be encompassed in the thinking process, resulting in some creative scenarios being developed. The thinking process provides a balance of thought between the logical analysis of factors and the intuitive sensing of issues by lateral thinking. Obtaining an outcome which uses the best of both components is what the enabler strives to accomplish.

Involving others in the process can significantly enhance the outputs if they are also prepared to 'let go' and create a future based on new constructs rather than what has been tried and tested in the past. This is not to say that we should not follow such definitive paths, rather we should not be locked into the safe and certain; mainly because the rate of change often means that what is effective today may not be as effective tomorrow. Enablers are aware of this phenomenon and thus use future visioning to keep an open mind to better solutions.

Shape the future

Being able to look forward with clarity is a valuable asset as it helps enablers shape the future. Much of their drive comes from the fact that they have a mission to their lives which has to do with moving forward. Enablers are people who enjoy life and have a desire to make a continuing contribution to their organization in particular and to society in general. Their mission can be expressed in the following statement:

> through my endeavours and vision of the future, I will develop and live by a philosophy which enables me to develop mean-

ingful and productive relationships with all whom I meet, resulting in an effective contribution to society.

Having a mission provides a focus which guides their lives and enables them to learn from experience and to apply the learning to shaping scenarios which can be tested against each set of emerging realities. Using creativity in solution-seeking has a high priority in enablers' thinking as it results in their being able to discover win/win solutions. This in turn generates an incentive for others to be excited about working with them. The excitement and enthusiasm which is generated has a great deal to do with quality of trust evident in each relationship.

Where trust exists in relationships, it provides a sound basis for people to take some risks. There is also a greater willingness to listen and be involved in activities which confront change in a positive manner. People are more willing to take new directions with enablers they trust. Their trust is considered valuable as it enables a climate of change to be perceived as one of opportunities which need to be developed. The enabler's sense of movement encourages individuals to be open and seek solutions to life's problems and opportunities.

ACHIEVEMENT ORIENTATION

The enablers' high concern for the people process was coupled with an equally determined and genuine desire to achieve. There was an inherent drive to develop clear goals which were expressed as expected observable/measurable outputs. Working within this goal orientation encouraged those involved to obtain a sharp focus on the part they could play and the contribution they could make.

Striving for achievement to appropriate standards is a positive position to take. It lets enablers share the benefits with others. Sharing is another observable characteristic displayed by an enabler and because people matter in this process of achieving, the enabler works at developing a sharing climate which encourages a high level of synergy to be realized.

Enablers, by their behaviour and forward movement, build confidence in individuals to be responsible for their actions. Taking charge of ourselves is a key factor in achieving results as we identify with the task, understand the contribution we can make and are committed to see it through to a successful conclusion.

In addition to having a clear purpose and direction the enabler looks for quality in all that is done. There is a belief in the ability of all to obtain high quality standards when it is an accepted part of the culture. The enabler's behaviour and actions support a culture of achievement within agreed quality standards. With such a model, enablers encourage individuals to learn by example and buy in to act in an appropriate manner because they really want to be part of a process which achieves for all.

To be an enabling leader we need a high level of awareness to enable us to test if our personal philosophy is creating the effect we desire. Being congruent is essential to our enabling activities and requires us to develop and fine tune our antennae to detect feedback which will help us keep on the right track. With a clear focus on the direction in which we are going, a willingness to make our contribution and ability to relate to others, we can achieve our goals.

The power of individuals making their unique contributions in a convergent direction is wonderful to observe as it generates the beliefs and energy which can move mountains. Although we may not regularly require mountains to be moved, we do need the energy, commitment and synergy to tackle the opportunities which would solve many of our organizational and societal problems. Application of this value is discussed in detail in Chapter 7 where we explore the role of achiever and orchestrator.

Commitment

We have no doubt that many readers already live by the values of enabling philosophy and use them to guide their lives. We also believe that individuals have an inherent desire to shape their lives to enable them to achieve fulfilment. By learning to accept and develop a personal philosophy in tune with the ideas expressed in this chapter, we can create an environment within which all can grow and develop. Enabling leadership creates an effective environment which encourages everyone to feel involved and committed to achieve in whatever field of service or endeavour they are engaged.

Having improved awareness and understood the values we use to guide our lives we are in an ideal position to make a commitment to be an enabler and allow others to benefit from our contribution. How we can improve ourselves and at the same time empower other individuals is described in Chapter 6 – Enabling learning.

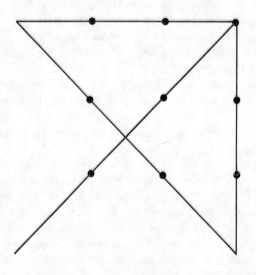

Figure 5.3   Nine dot puzzle (2)

CONCEPTS EXPLORED IN CHAPTER 6

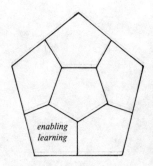

enabling
learning

6 Enabling learning

REVISITING LEARNING AND DEVELOPMENT

We are excited about the changes taking place in the arena of learning and development around the world. This is primarily a result of the need to equip individuals to be effective in a variety of new situations caused by the speed of change which is likely to accelerate as we move further into the future. Individuals need to develop and acquire new attitudes, skills and knowledge to enable them to cope with the challenge of ambiguity, uncertainty, excitement and new opportunities which the future may offer.

How individuals are developed has a significant impact on their contribution to the organizations with which they are involved. Many practitioners engaged in the human resource development field have become increasingly aware of the inadequacy of much of the learning and development activities offered. On analyzing output from learning events it becomes clear that there is still a tendency to provide an experience which relates more to the past than to the future. The design of learning is still based on using components which fail to meet the needs of a large number of learners:

- standardization
- conformity
- rote learning
- specialized syllabuses
- rigid timetables

- individual and competitive
- linear thinking
- examination driven.

These do not generally create an environment which releases talent and encourages individuals to want to learn. The way forward is to change methods of learning which constrain the natural and potential development capabilities of individuals. Young children are exciting examples of this potential as they 'discover' and acquire attitudes, skills and knowledge. That is, until their attention and energy is focused on passing exams, at which stage their learning capabilities begin to be inhibited.

The way forward

This chapter on enabling learning offers a constructive process which captures the best of what exists in learning practice and technology and then adds to it ideas which will enhance its value in the future. It is about creating a purpose and environment which enables every individual to make an effective contribution irrespective of age, social, economic, environmental, physical and mental capacities.

Learning is the pivot on which awareness and philosophy can be turned into positive action. Enablers express consistent views on the importance of learning: firstly, as a process of acquiring attitudes, skills and knowledge; secondly, in developing their philosophy; thirdly, as a process for enabling others to develop and achieve. They talk about learning with pleasure and highlight the following four attitudes:

- keen interest in learning as a development process
- learning to be self-managed
- taking risks in disclosure/feedback
- learning as a life-long process.

Enablers display a constructive interest in learning as a means of developing their attitudes, skills and knowledge. Also, they confound the theory that the more senior people are in an organization the less inclined they appear to be in developing themselves. In the cases studied we discovered that enablers at all levels in organizations were motivated to learn and develop as a means of improving their performance.

The second observation was how much of their development activities were self managed. It was a powerful experience to learn how enablers had interwoven developing their awareness and personal philosophies with a self-directed learning orientation. The desire to learn more about themselves was strong and was expressed through their willingness to disclose thoughts and feelings. Being sensitive and open to others provides an arena for individuals to understand them better and also encourages honest feedback on performance. Facilitating the feedback/disclosure loop is a part of the enabler's process which is achieved in a climate of sharing with individuals growing from the experience.

This led to the third observation, the degree of risk enablers take when developing their own performance and in encouraging others to develop. We witnessed interactions with enablers which contained very high levels of disclosure within an environment of trust. Parts of the information could be considered sensitive if used out of context. Yet we found time and again enablers prepared to take calculated risks as a means of obtaining a better understanding of themselves with the specific purpose of improving their performance. A similar process applied when they provided feedback to others in a manner designed to raise awareness and enable individuals to obtain an 'objective' picture of themselves.

Life-long learning was the fourth outcome we observed. In all cases enablers saw learning as a continuous process. It is an important part of their lives and is perceived to be central to the development of their enabling skills. They view every interaction as an opportunity to gain insights and practise enabling.

Enablers weave the attitudes together to form a determined and sensitive approach to learning in all its aspects. Although we heard of many concerns about current approaches to learning, the general outlook was positive in the belief that they could influence change for the better.

We decided to focus on adult learning in this chapter as the book is aimed at an adult readership. However, we are aware that most of what we write is just as applicable to the development of young people.

The whole person

An outcome of research into learning has been an increasing awareness of how it should be structured to meet the needs of the whole person. At present these can be described as an individual's mental, physical, social and spiritual needs. Recognizing the need to devise learning in a way which develops the whole person has provided a major stimulus to the development of learning materials and processes. I mentioned earlier that it was our own research which led us to explore and then adopt the concept of enabling. To us the enabling concept embraces developing the whole person.

To provide us with a framework by which we could examine and modify our approach to learning design and practice, we constructed the following model of learning. Inputs to the model have come from a wide range of enablers and individuals involved in organizational and personal development activities over the past five years in particular. Many of the specific inputs have come from 'ah ha's': the sudden realization of what it is all about that makes sense to the individual. We are grateful for the generous sharing of insights as these have helped us to understand the learning process.

To give you a picture of the enabling learning model, we listed ten of its assumptions and compared them with assumptions drawn from traditional learning models (Figure 6.1).

By developing the enabling learning model we do not intend to dismiss traditional learning models. We recognize that they fulfil the need of some people in an effective manner. However, when we explored learning styles it became obvious that traditional learning models fail to meet the learning needs of a significant number of people. In our view traditional learning can be enhanced by adopting the outputs of enabling learning.

As we studied how enablers approached the process of learning we found that they tended to use an integrated process. Although

	Enabling learning *assumptions*	*Traditional learning* *assumptions*
1	*the aim of learning is to stimulate a person to want to learn and this release the person's innate potential*	*the aim of learning is to fill the empty vessel, as typified by the 'mug and jug' syndrome*
2	*learning is enhanced within an environment which creates a desire in individuals to seek knowledge and understanding*	*learning is about imparting a body of useful knowledge to the learner*
3	*intelligence is developed as a learner develops the capacity to learn*	*intelligence is measured by the learner's ability to absorb knowledge*
4	*learning is enhanced when it is designed to meet a person's specific needs*	*learning is effectivewhen it follows a well tried standard and uniform procedure*
5	*learning can be enjoyable and achieved within an environment of collaboration*	*learning is hard work, serious and involves a process stimulated by a competitive environment*
6	*learning is concerned with developing the whole person*	*learning is concerned with affecting factors which influence external behaviours*
7	*combining analytical with intuitive thinking will encourage a learner to use a multitude of skills and experiences to learn*	*the most effective skills, associated with effective learning come from rational and analytical thinking*
8	*learning will be enhanced when learners experience learning at many different levels at once*	*learning is effective when the learner deals with single topics in a sequential manner*
9	*learners are encouraged to perceive the whole and enhance their understanding by exploring the parts*	*learning is achieved by encouraging learners to study the parts to obtain a picture of the whole*
10	*learning takes place during the duration of a learner's life*	*learning effectiveness is at its peak during the first 15 years of a person's life*

Figure 6.1   Enabling learning model

the process is integrated, we managed to differentiate the following six stages:

Stage 1
    create a learning environment and culture which encourages learner-directed and paced development

Stage 2
    encourage individuals to identify and express their learning expectations/learning goals in observable/measurable terms

Stage 3
    develop content, identify resources to be used, and relate to learning styles

Stage 4
    agree groundrules to cover the learning activity plus the degree of involvement/assistance required from others

Stage 5
    develop performance standards and feedback processes to enable progress to be assessed and modifications to learning made as required

Stage 6
    undertake the learning activity using feedback from stage 5 to assist modifications to enable goals to be achieved/modified in light of changed circumstances, and to know when learning has finished and the behaviours internalized.

Experience shows that the six stages are used as an integrated process rather than as discrete and sequential units. This accounts for the dynamic nature of learning which takes place on many different levels and involves many different aspects of an individual's development. The stages provide a focus which enables individuals to think through what they want to achieve and helps them obtain a clear understanding of what is expected and how it can be achieved.

An enabler's primary aim is to encourage individuals to be responsible for their own learning, development and growth. Moving to establish a learning process which encourages a learner-directed approach can produce significant benefits for learners with responsibility for learning being clearly placed with them. This is not to propose that the learner should be left in a 'sink or swim' situation. What is required is a commitment from the learner to invest time and energy in a learning activity. Assistance will be given in a sensitive and aware manner to help individuals understand the benefits. They will be aware of what is involved and clearly understand it is their responsibility to provide motivation and commitment. Given a learner's willingness to be involved in learning, we now explore the six stages to see how learning is enabled.

STAGE 1 – LEARNING ENVIRONMENT

Creating the environment

The enabling learning model describes the characteristics and assumptions which are used to construct a learning environment. A key objective is associated with encouraging individuals to learn to manage their own learning. Enablers perceive this to be a major outcome from the process of empowering.

We recognized early in our research the fundamental benefit of self-directed learning. When learners manage their own learning they have an increasing ability to modify an environment to meet their needs. This transfer of responsibility for shaping a learning environment is a healthy move as it now places the onus on both enabler and learner. Within a collaborative learning environment, the learner will aim to reach agreement on the following issues:

- what needs to be learned
- the rate of learning
- where learning will take place
- what will be used to assist learning
- who will assist in the process and what role they will be invited to perform
- how the content will be structured/not structured to meet learning needs
- how progress will be assessed
- how learning will be related to the real world

- what can be done to reinforce positively that which has been learned and found to be effective.

Many of the issues will be covered within the different stages of the learning process described above. However, it is worth noting that in a dynamic process the issues will not slot neatly into each phase. Rather, within an enabling learning environment where learning is multi-dimensional, each of the issues can be addressed during different stages of the process. This enables the learner to be involved in many different learning experiences. Armed with understandable learning goals, and being flexible and open to change, is a sound basis on which a learner can develop learning to meet specific needs.

Learning continuum

Aiming to achieve effective outputs from learning is one of the main driving forces experienced by both learner and enabler. Given that both are clear what outputs are expected, their relative roles in the process can then be agreed. Reference to the learning continuum will indicate where the learner is positioned at different times during the process (Figure 6.2).

The enablers' aim is to assist the learners to manage their own learning as quickly as possible. Benefits from a self-managed

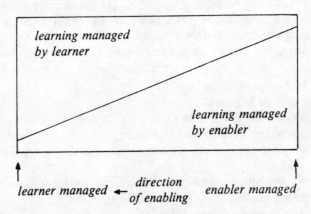

Figure 6.2   Learning continuum

process can provide additional stimulus for learners to want to continue the process once original goals have been reached.

Self-managed learning

An encouraging aspect of people development is the increasing number of enablers in business, commerce and government who recognize the value of self-managed learning. We meet an increasing number of managers, teachers, trainers and individuals who are actively involved in developing learning environments which provide development opportunities on a learner-managed basis. Within a learner-managed environment, the learner is learning how to learn in a way which makes effective use of available resources and seeks out new resources to achieve desired results. The environment encourages each individual to use a high level of creativity, be curious and willing to learn through a process of study, guidance, discovery and experimentation. Most real learning comes from being aware of what enables individuals to be successful and sometimes unsuccessful.

The environment which enablers strive to create provides individuals with scope to understand what is involved and how it can be undertaken. Such an environment will encourage them to:

- decide what needs to be learned
- manage the acquisition of ASK (attitudes, skills and knowledge): self-pacing
- adapt/modify plans as 'need to know' becomes evident
- decide what internal/external rewards and recognition are appropriate to reflect achievement
- maintain a focus on the real world in which they need to relate and be effective
- select methods, techniques and vehicles to facilitate learning
- transact with others to secure assistance as required.

As enablers become involved in assisting individuals to learn and shape their own learning process, they need to be able to disengage from wanting to help from the 'we know what's best for them' attitude. Although enablers may be 'correct' in their assessment, they are aware of how easy it is to create a dependent relationship, through telling and directing, with the learner.

The main aim is to develop an environment which allows the learner the freedom to decide on what should be done whether it results in success or failure. Inputs and guidance are provided as information to enable individuals to perceive the risks involved. If an individual wishes to attempt a risky adventure which could result in either a painful or exciting experience, the possible consequences will be better understood at the beginning.

The enabling environment encourages an individual to take risks based on awareness of the potential results. Being able to experiment with the aim of succeeding, yet not achieving the results expected, can provide significant learning for the next attempt. The enabling environment does not judge an individual's attempt as a success or failure. It provides an opportunity for the individual to receive objective feedback on the attempt. Providing opportunities for individuals to explore learning and to understand their needs provides an effective foundation on which they can build and develop.

Learning to improve performance

For learning to be effective, enablers recognize the need to develop a process which encourages individuals to think about what they seek to achieve from a learning experience. Although this may appear to be a relatively easy request to make, from experience many individuals have considerable difficulty envisioning and expressing what they hope to achieve beyond an initially superficial level. This is partly due to the passive nature experienced with most formal learning where direction and guidance on what should be learned is provided by the institution. It also applies in many organizations where learning needs are identified by the manager, teacher, trainer, lecturer. These perceived needs are described as the attitudes, skill and knowledge required by an individual to do a particular job, task or activity. Once identified the learning content is determined by the organization, and the event is structured to meet those perceived needs.

Organizations are still producing training packages to meet training needs identified by those in authority without the involvement of the individuals concerned. Individuals are processed through the package in standard and uniform ways with effectiveness being assessed by testing what the individuals have learned. Feedback on the events often includes comments on how the person felt about the facilities, the lecturer/trainer, the content and its delivery. However, trainers are often left with a nagging uncertainty about the value of the training provided. Our research into transfer of learning from classroom to the workplace indicates that much of the training has a minimum impact on subsequent on-the-job performance, except where learners have a clear understanding of what will be different in their performance following the event.

STAGE 2 – LEARNING EXPECTATIONS AND GOALS

Enablers work to overcome the problem by encouraging individuals to think about their learning needs. This involves inviting them to think about why they should be involved in learning. When individuals express a wish to learn, an enabler will encourage them to identify what triggered their desire and what they expect to achieve. Individuals who are perceived to need development, but do not see this for themselves, need to be involved in a process which helps them, firstly, to understand what others perceive their learning needs to be and, secondly, to give them the choice of what to do. The aim is to involve individuals with the purpose of gaining agreement and commitment to learn as a means of improving performance.

This part of the enabling learning process has the following four steps which are designed to assist individuals obtain a clear understanding of the outcomes expected from a particular learning activity:

First step
  identify the reasons why they want to, or should, undertake a particular learning activity

Second step
  encourage them to describe what will be different on completion of the learning activity

Third step
   identify what needs to be learned to achieve step 2 above

Fourth step
   describe the learning goals identified in step 3 in observable/measurable output terms.

> From our research we have established that many individuals have some difficulty in developing clearly stated and understandable learning goals. We have also observed the remarkable difference in learning outcomes which are achieved by learners who have a clear awareness compared with others who do not.
>
> To help readers to examine the concept, we explore in detail how to develop observable/measurable learning goals using a person we call Joanne as an example. Joanne is a woman in her mid-thirties and manager of an accounts department in a large retail organization. This is how she worked her way through the various steps.

First step – Why be involved?

The first step involves the enabler in encouraging an individual to tease out the issues with a view to understanding the circumstances which stimulate the person to want to learn. This is a most important step in the process.

> During Joanne's annual performance review she expressed a desire to be more aggressive/assertive. When exploring the idea with an enabler she was encouraged to think about the reasons she wanted to become more assertive. After some thought and sharing of ideas, the following reason was identified:
>
> • I am becoming increasingly uncomfortable at management meetings as I feel unable to present my case in a convincing manner.

The enabler continued the discussion to seek what had triggered her desire to change. After some thought she identified the triggers as being:

- I am a member of a management team of six in which I am the only woman
- although my colleagues are about the same age, their management experience is considerably greater than mine
- when I present information to support something required for my department I feel that my colleagues are quick to discount my need if it conflicts with something they want
- I perceive that the colleagues who achieve most are those who present their case in a strong and aggressive manner.

The enabler invited Joanne to examine each of the factors to check if she had made any assumptions. She responded by agreeing that the first trigger was factual whereas in the other three she had made a number of assumptions. On closer examination Joanne admitted that she really did not know if the men had more experience than her. She had based the assessment on the fact that they had all been managers longer than her. In the process Joanne had not placed much weight on the four years she had been second in command of the finance department before being appointed manager.

She also recognized a reason her colleagues may not have given her views much air time was due to the poor way she presented her case. She occasionally felt ill at ease when centre stage during a meeting. Joanne also believed that she had been mistaken in thinking that aggression achieved the best results after reflecting on who actually was the most effective manager. She concluded that Robert achieved most and did so in a quiet, assured and assertive manner whilst displaying respect for the views of others.

Second step – What would be different?

Now that some of the main triggers have been identified the enabler and Joanne moved on to the second step. This requires her to describe what would be different when she became more assertive. Her initial response was to say that she wanted to withstand the pressure she felt from her colleagues.

Joanne was asked to reconsider her initial response and to imagine what she would *do* differently at a subsequent management meeting. Particularly if she was seeking approval for resources which could place her in conflict with colleagues. Joanne described what she wanted to do:

- feel calm and in control of my emotions, be fully prepared to respond to any questions asked and be able to describe the benefits to be gained from use of the resources
- feel confident and assured when presenting information
- be able to manage conflict in a way which leaves colleagues and myself feeling comfortable by making it a win/win negotiation
- learn to project myself at all times so that my voice and body language demonstrate my emotions are under control.

Satisfied with the outcomes expressed Joanne explored what she would need to learn to enable her to fulfil the scenario drawn. This thought about her present behaviour and how this differed from what she wanted to achieve. To help her obtain a clear picture the enabler suggested that she develop a learning needs profile.

	learning need	level of effectiveness low 1 2 3 4 5 6 7 8 9 10 high
a	able fully to prepare case to support project	● at 7, ○ at 9
b	able to present my case in a confident and assured manner	● at 5, ○ at 7
c	able to negotiate with colleagues to achieve win/win outcome	● at 5, ○ at 7
d	competent in managing conflict	● at 5, ○ at 6
e	project self in a consistent way at all times	● at 7, ○ at 9
f	be able to control my emotions	● at 5, ○ at 9

Figure 6.3 **Learning needs profile (1)**

Drawing from the scenario Joanne was able to list six components which cover her main learning needs. She assessed the level of her current performance by marking an 'x' at the appropriate point. She then identified the actual level of performance to meet her need to be assertive and recorded this with an 'o' on the profile. Joanne's completed profile is shown in Figure 6.3.

Having completed the profile Joanne was asked to identify particular attitudes, knowledge and skills required to enable her to behave in the way described in her output scenario.

She reflected on the question, and in discussion with the enabler, said that she needed more time to think about the meaning of her learning needs profile. She felt she needed to be more aware of how her colleagues perceived her performance and how this compared with her self-perception.

She would use the learning needs profile as a basis to discuss with colleagues with whom she felt comfortable, and with several senior members of her department with whom she had a good relationship.

Joanne agreed to meet the enabler in two weeks' time, by when she would have clarified her thinking in relation to the work they had done during the learning needs analysis session. She also said that she would attempt to identify specific skills associated with each of her learning needs.

Third step – What do I need to learn?

Joanne studied the learning needs profile to see if she could obtain a better understanding of what it meant. She drew lines connecting the 'x's and the 'o's to produce a profile of the 'now' and the 'future'. She then recorded on the profile a number which represented the perceived gap in her learning. The result of this analysis is shown in Figure 6.4.

On further examination Joanne recognized that items f, e and b all related to how she wanted to project herself and this was identified as her primary learning need. She also saw that items c and d could be linked together and would be her second learning need. Item a, although important, was not a

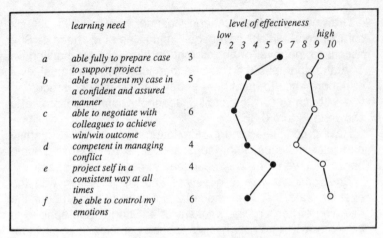

Figure 6.4   Learning needs profile (2)

high priority as her performance in this area was already of an acceptable standard.

Joanne subsequently had a number of discussions with colleagues and staff to share the analysis work she had done. Feedback clearly indicted that her analysis of learning needs had been reasonably accurate. Comments supported the view that during discussions she tended to become emotional if her views were challenged or if she appeared to be on thin ice. However, Joanne was pleased to learn from the feedback that people accepted her as being competent in performing her job.

Joanne felt comfortable in being able to glean what skills she would require to learn in order to achieve the performance standard required. She prepared a list of the specific learning areas to discuss with the enabler. After discussion and clarifying she felt the following list presented a realistic picture of what she wanted to achieve and what she needed to learn:

● I want to be competent in presenting a case in a confident and assured manner with the ability to control my emotions and thus be consistent in how I relate to others. This will require me to learn the following:
   presentation skills
   self-awareness
   relaxation techniques

voice projection
image projection (dress and posture)
understanding attitudes and behaviour
empathy and flexibility

- I want to negotiate with colleagues to achieve results which are recognized as win/win by being able to understand others' needs and manage potential conflict situations:
  win/win transaction skills
  understanding stress and its impact
  use of time
  conflict resolution
  participative management
  use of power and influence

- I want to develop my skills in preparing and writing materials to support my case:
  report writing
  decision-making
  problem-solving
  creativity.

Although the list initially appeared formidable, Joanne recognized that she already possessed a degree of knowledge and skills in most cases. Her needs in some areas could be met by a review of current learning materials whereas in other areas she would need assistance. With her growing awareness of what she now wanted to learn to achieve her objectives, Joanne moved on to the fourth step in the analysis process.

Fourth step – How do I measure learning needs?

To complete this part of the process Joanne was invited to describe what she wanted to learn within each of the areas described above. She initially focused on presentation skills and after a brainstorming session, produced the following list:

- I would want to acquire the following knowledge and skills about presentation

- techniques used to present information such as reports, overhead projection, slide projection, flip-chart, white board, video, audio visual
- how to prepare visual aids to enable information to be communicated in an effective manner either visually in a presentation or contained in a report
- techniques which can be used to project confidence and self-assurance with ability to handle questions, discussion, debate, interruptions and confrontation
- learning to listen, identify and understand the needs of others involved in the presentation
- how to manage the presentation process to enable me to present my case whilst allowing others to feel part of the process
- understanding how to create an environment which enables people to give adequate attention during my presentation.

Joanne was asked to think about how she would recognize when she had acquired the level of skill and knowledge which she desired. Did she feel that the statements listed above provided her with sufficient information to enable her to assess standards of performance? Joanne was reasonably satisfied with the results so far and wondered what else could be done to make them more specific. The enabler asked her to describe what would tell her that she had acquired the learning she was seeking; furthermore, what she would do differently from what she already did. Joanne responded by stating that from the second item on the presentation skills list she needed to be able to:

• prepare visual aids in a way which presents the information in readily understandable form by being able to select from text, charts and diagrams; when to use 'self-made' or 'professionally' prepared material; how to decide on the medium to be used to communicate the information, e.g. reports, memo, newsletter, face to face, flip-chart
• use an overhead projector confidently by knowing how to switch on/off, position it, change bulbs, fix screen, adjust focus, use transparencies, use scroll film.

By this time, Joanne was very satisfied with the analysis of what would be different and understood that she could continue to identify further specific components. She recognized the importance of being satisfied that the information developed was in sufficient detail to enable her to set performance standards against which she could assess progress. How this is done is discussed in stage 5 of the learning process.

As individuals work through the first two stages in the enabling learning process they should be able to identify much of the content of what they need to learn. Therefore, the primary aim of the analysis process is to provide detail of what individuals should seek to learn in terms of content in order to meet their learning goals. The value of investing time at this stage should be recognized as it provides a useful method for assessing the relevance of what is on offer from providers of learning materials and resources.

STAGE 3 – CONTENT, RESOURCES AND LEARNING STYLES

The difficulty of determining what a person requires to learn is often overstated. Enablers accept that learning takes place on a continuous basis. Quite often, when individuals identify a learning need and research what they need to acquire, they recognize that parts already exist to the standard required. By understanding the fluid nature of learning, individuals can be relaxed about identifying needs by being willing to explore acquiring them in an open and sensitive manner.

With an open and creative enabling environment individuals learn to approach the analysis of learning needs as an interesting and effective vehicle for testing understanding. It often comes as a surprise to individuals involved in learning to have a dawning realization of how well they can perform. This reinforces our belief in the value of providing individuals with the opportunity to explore the content of a particular learning activity prior to involvement. They can obtain a clear understanding of what the learning opportunity offers, in addition to becoming aware of knowledge and skills which they already possess. It can also provide valuable inputs for the educators/trainers in terms of how they can modify the learning activity to meet specific needs of an individual. Modification could include developing learning vehicles to be used by individuals in a self-managed process.

Identifying resources required

Having a detailed picture of the content of each learning activity provides individuals with the opportunity to compare needs with available learning resources. At the present time the majority of individuals who seek some form of learning and development have a number of options open to them which can include:

- attending a formal course run by an educational authority within a school, college, polytechnic or university
- attending a course run by a professional body or commercial organization
- studying at home using a distance-learning approach such as those offered by correspondence colleges, Open Tech, Open University, Open College
- attending a company-sponsored course which could be either on or off the job
- making use of self-managed learning materials such as books, cassettes, audio/visual programmes, video cassettes, textbooks and computer-based learning
- individual instruction/tuition from manager, coach, tutor, mentor, and from other individual experiences such as job rotation, secondment, project group assignment, observation and role modelling
- belonging to a self-development group which meets with the purpose of providing individuals with the opportunity to build confidence and enhance their learning capability.

Many of these resources offer excellent opportunities for individuals to acquire the desired learning input. Having clear learning goals enables individuals to be highly selective in deciding on the resource which best meets their need. As society moves from traditional learning to enabling learning many resources will develop to become more learner-oriented and provide a greater degree of flexibility in meeting individual needs. Attitudes to learning will also change as individuals recognize a need to be flexible and adaptable to meet changing world, society, community and individual requirements.

Individuals will have the confidence to select a particular resource which best meets their needs. If it is not available, they will be able to secure the resources required through win/win negotiations. The change in focus to individually managed learning will require major changes in many of the organizations who are providers of learning resources. However, the opposite is also true in that people who have the freedom to choose their learning medium will be more tolerant in accepting some of what is provided by organizations at present.

The enabling approach is designed to weld a partnership between the individual learner and the provider of a learning resource. This partnership leads to a higher level of sensitivity and awareness, by both parties, of what is required and what can be provided within current resources and technology. It also exemplifies a willingness to develop new and improved methods of enhancing the learning process to meet individual learning styles.

Learning styles

During the past five years significant developments into learning styles have taken place resulting in recognition that people learn in different ways. This is highlighted through the dissatisfaction enablers feel at the way many people are processed through uniform and standardized systems of learning. Within this mechanistic process, everyone is subjected to similar and standardized inputs irrespective of their individual learning preferences. The assumption is that individual learning preferences can in fact be shaped through exposure to fit this defined and regulated learning model. Assumption 4 of the Traditional Learning model would be used to support the practice described above. However, enablers have been increasingly aware of the need to provide learning activities which can be adapted by individuals to meet their own learning styles.

To help us understand how to identify learning styles we

embarked on a project to uncover learning preferences displayed by different individuals. During the past four years our focus has been on studying the learning styles of individuals involved in our learning activities. We introduced a process which invited participants to identify learning expectations and goals prior to attending a learning activity. This was followed by a discussion about how they would prefer the learning activity to be structured. From the discussions we identified learning preferences and started to construct a model which enabled us to understand learning styles.

During this period we began using a computer-based programme designed to identify communication styles used by individuals, as perceived by others. We became aware that the computer feedback on communication and social styles provided close correlation with the learning styles and preferences displayed by individuals who participated in subsequent awareness skills learning events. Following further exploration we were able to identify four styles which we feel represent the main learning preferences used by individuals involved in our learning activities.

As our research continues, we expect to add to our findings and develop methods which enable individuals to identify their own learning style. In the meantime we share brief details of the four styles (Figure 6.5).

try it and see	*flow with the group*
let's get on with the task	*one step at a time*

Figure 6.5   Learning styles

Try it and see learning style

A person who enjoys the excitement of experimenting with new ideas and who approaches learning from an experiential and conceptual base. This person has the capacity to visualize and be creative in developing learning to meet his/her needs. A person who is equally happy working on an individual project or as part of a group activity. Learning will be enhanced by providing the opportunity for experimentation, feedback, recognition and challenge.

Flow with the group learning style

A person who enjoys the pleasure of being part of a group-learning experience and who approaches learning using intuition, feeling and creativity. This person has the capacity to integrate with others and obtain their support and cooperation in the learning process. A person who likes to be involved, shares ideas and feels learning as an intrinsic experience. Learning will be enhanced by active involvement in groups coupled with the use of music, movement and harmony.

One step at a time learning style

A person who enjoys dealing with all the facts associated with what needs to be learned. This person wants to test theories in a structured way within well defined boundaries. He/she will want to take each issue one step at a time and explore each component as a means of building the whole picture. A person who likes to attend lectures and study from textbooks as an effective means of building knowledge and know how. Learning will be enhanced by the provision of information in structured form with opportunities for the individual to test understanding with informed and intelligent people

Let's get on with the task learning style

A person who wants to achieve the best result possible with an effective use of time and effort. This person learns by exploring ideas in a logical fashion with a desire to see a practical application at the end of the learning process. He/she values facts and enjoys discussing the issues in a logical and precise manner as long as a practical outcome is achieved. Learning will be enhanced through formal study, programmed learning, and methods which enable the person to achieve results in an effective manner.

It is important to understand that we do not envisage an individual fitting precisely into a particular learning style. The development of the model is to provide a framework which enables individuals to understand why they appear to respond more positively to particular learning activities. Having this understanding enables them to identify ways in which they can modify their style to suit the learning process or, alternatively, to attempt to modify the learning process to better suit their style.

Once individuals are aware of their learning style preferences, they begin to understand which vehicles they can use to learn effectively. They also recognize that their style preference may also contain some of the characteristics from other styles due to their past learning experiences. We perceive that the 80:20 rule applies which indicates that 80 per cent of the style describes fairly well the actual majority preference an individual has. From feedback received, individuals say that an awareness of learning preferences has been valuable in assisting them understand what to do to improve their learning capability.

An enabler's aim is to be proactive in developing materials and resources to meet the changing needs of individuals. In addition, they also aim to encourage and equip individuals with the skills and ability to develop their own learning materials and influence providers of learning resources to be more responsive to their needs.

STAGE 4 – SEEKING ASSISTANCE AND AGREEING GROUNDRULES

As individuals become more aware of what they need to learn they will be able to select the most appropriate resource to meet their learning needs. The enabler's role within this process will be one of transferring responsibility for learning from the institution to the individual. Many individuals will experience little difficulty in accepting this responsibility as they have acquired skills of awareness and direction to their lives. Others, who have been subjected to a higher level of dependency, may require developmental coaching/counselling to enable them to make the transition.

We observe a transformation in the learning process and delivery as learning takes on a more enabling approach and learning environments become more responsive to the needs of individual learners. The early stages of the transformation can be detected through the increasing numbers becoming involved in self-managed learning and development coupled with a positive response by institutions to modify their delivery to meet this new and more discerning market.

Learning relationship

One outcome of the transformation will be in the relationship between learner and teacher. Enabling leadership plays a significant role in encouraging educators/trainers and others interested in the learning process and delivery to explore the assumptions expressed in the enabling learning model. The emphasis is on exploration, exchanging, and sharing to reach an understanding of the implications of adapting learning to meet the assumptions of the model. The process which managers, trainers, teachers, parents and individuals require to experience may be similar to the process for a person becoming an enabling leader.

They need to identify with the mission of their particular learning organization and modify as required their behaviour and actions to meet its philosophy and objectives. One of the most important values is respect for the individual and this can be positively reinforced by developing a relationship of equals during the learning process. This acknowledges that at some point during the process the enabler may have much more to share with the learner. However, in an open and equal relationship the enabler often obtains as much benefit from the learner. Being aware and open to learn from each learning transaction can provide mutually beneficial and fulfilling experiences.

When a learner identifies the need to seek assistance from another person they aim to agree together how that person can be of assistance. This is done in a number of ways including the following:

- agreeing groundrules to cover the learning relationship
- establishing a learning agreement.

Groundrules

In the former situation learners establish ground rules in discussion with the person or organization from whom they are seeking assistance. The process they use is similar to the one we describe in Chapter 7. The list of items developed by the parties could include the following:

- how assistance will be provided
  - face to face
  - by telephone
  - correspondence
  - tape recorder/video
  - resource materials
  - networking
  - computers

- timeframe and frequency of involvement
  - location
  - feedback process
  - performance review process

- standards of performance
  - how the standards will be expressed
  - how feedback will be given
  - what will be the monitoring process.

The purpose of developing groundrules is to provide a clear and understandable framework within which the parties can operate. As the learning activity progresses any information and insights which indicate the ground rules need to change are discussed and modified appropriately. This provides a sound basis on which the learning relationship can function effectively.

Learning agreement

When using the term 'agreement' the intention is to indicate a specific arrangement between two or more parties. Recently this has become a technique used to obtain clear understanding and commitment of the individual involved to a significant learning activity. In our experience a learning agreement has been associated with the following learning and development activities:

- management development programme for recently appointed graduates
- job rotation assignment prior to major promotion
- attendance on a twelve-week learning course at a major business school.

We are aware of examples of oral agreements which provide a sound foundation on which development outputs have been understood and achieved. The value in producing a written agreement comes from the fact that some individuals prefer hard copy text. They need to see what has been agreed: this allows them to refer to its content as learning progresses.

Therefore the learning agreement is a process for obtaining a clear understanding of what is required and obtaining a definite commitment from the individuals involved to put the necessary energy and drive into achieving results.

STAGE 5 – PERFORMANCE STANDARDS AND FEEDBACK

Allowing for the dynamic nature of learning, it is essential for enablers to attempt to establish standards against which individual performance can be assessed. Establishing performance standards provides the individual, and others involved in the learning activity, with a clear understanding of what has to be achieved.

The initial phase involves working to determine how the standard can be accurately described and then how to obtain feedback on whether it is being achieved. Therefore individuals decide what standard provides objective feedback on performance. Being aware of what they are attempting to learn, and understanding how well they are progressing, is essential to the learning process. When we refer to standards of performance we understand that these are standards established by the *learner*.

A particular standard may be reached following consultation with the provider of a learning resource or other interested person such as a coach. However, we feel it is a central part of self-managed learning to encourage the learner to set and be responsible for achieving realistic performance standards. When standards are perceived by others as unambitious/overambitious, it is valid for the observer to share with the learner in an enabling way. However, the final choice would still remain with the learner.

For example, if we return to the place where we left Joanne, we could see how she subsequently developed her learning goals to include standards which could be assessed (Figure 6.6).

STAGE 6 – LEARNING AND KNOWING WHEN IT IS ACCOMPLISHED

Knowing what they aim to achieve from a learning activity and having established performance standards, enables learners to seek feedback on how well they are performing. In many instances they can obtain direct feedback by observing and assessing their own performance against the established standards. However, in other instances, they can benefit from receiving objective feedback from others. This provides learners with the opportunity to test their understanding of actual performance with the observations and assessment of other interested individuals. When performance is to an agreed standard, learners can then act with confidence using the new learning.

As they practise their new ASK and fine tune those parts which do not produce the desired results they will internalize the learning and operate increasingly on autopilot. When feedback indicates that learners are having difficulty it provides them with an opportunity to:

- seek further help
- re-examine the goals and performance standards to see if they need to be modified

Learning goals and standard of performance		
1 *prepare visual aids*	*measurable*	*observable*
■ *present information in understandable form*		●
produce charts and diagrams		
able to draw and use text and graphics		
to a standard where people comment on		
their acceptable quality	●	
■ *decide on self-made or professionally prepared*		
able to identify the factors which influence		
the audience		●
be aware of the cost/benefit equation		
in terms of time and effort required		●
■ *assess listener's response to either choice*		●
decide on medium to be used		
ability to identify needs of audience		
in terms of time, location, numbers,		
culture and outputs required		●
2 *confidently use overhead projector*		
■ *set up projector, plug in and connect power*	●	
set up viewing surface	●	
switch power on/off	●	
change projector bulb	●	
adjust focus	●	
fit transparencies	●	
■ *write/draw legibly on scroll to enable*		
audience comfortably to view the data		●
■ *manage the presentation by knowing how long*		
to display transparencies and when to switch		
projector off/on		●
■ *how to use mask, pointer and pin light to*		
focus audience attention on key points		●
■ *be able to perform all the actions in a*		
comfortable and intuitive manner		●

Figure 6.6 Learning goals and standard of performance

- explore different learning vehicles to see if they can assist
- obtain additional feedback on performance from other individuals who may be able to offer different perspectives to add to the learning process.

When individuals are invited to be involved and give feedback, it makes sense to provide them with an objective framework against which they can provide relevant feedback. The more detail in which we express the expected outputs from learning the better equipped another person will be to provide effective feedback. And to ensure the learning relationship continues in an effective manner, the learner will need to establish appropriate ground rules to enable disclosure and feedback to be handled in a sensitive and enabling way.

The end result of a learning process should be the successful acquisition of the desired attitudes, skills and knowledge. Learners feel good at having achieved and are motivated to maintain and improve performance. When they reach a high level of performance the new ASK learned will become a part of their normal behaviour.

AN ENABLING CULTURE

As enablers encourage the development of self-managed learning, they need to examine carefully the values, beliefs and assumptions individuals hold about learning. In Chapter 5, we explore the concept of Enabling Philosophy and express the view that an enabling leader would accept the majority of its values. We hold a similar view in relation to Enabling Learning as those involved in the learning process need to agree its mission and develop the values on which an effective self-managed learning culture can be constructed.

If society is to achieve the maximum benefit from its human resources, it will need to provide an enabling learning environment. This should result in a dynamic process which produces individuals able to cope with and adapt to change, and make a significant contribution to the development of an effective and caring society as envisioned in Chapter 2.

We believe the key concepts of enabling awareness, philosophy and learning, form the foundations and architecture on which an effective way of life can be constructed. An exciting part of the process is in the freedom an individual has to interpret the concepts and build their own enabling shape. However, whatever shape emerges it will need to be congruent with the Enabling

Leadership concept. The next part of the book, examines how enablers 'add value' to achieve effective outputs in whatever activity they are involved.

Part III
ENABLING OUTPUTS

Explores the attitudes, skills and knowledge employed by enabling leaders to create an environment of positive achievement

Chapter 7 ENABLING ROLES
    TRANSACTING
    ENABLING ROLES
    UNDERSTANDING COMMUNICATOR ROLE
    ACHIEVER AND ORCHESTRATOR ROLE
    SOLUTION-SEEKER ROLE
    COACH ROLE
    DEVELOPMENTAL COUNSELLOR ROLE

Chapter 8 ENABLING PROCESS (1) – Enabling organization
    AN ENABLING ORGANIZATION
    ORGANIZATIONAL MISSION
    ORGANIZATIONAL CULTURE
    SHARED VALUES
    DEVELOPING INDIVIDUALS AND TEAMS

Chapter 9 ENABLING PROCESS (2) – Enabling contribution
    ENABLING CONTRIBUTION
    INDIVIDUAL CONTRIBUTOR
    STRATEGY
    AIMS AND OBJECTIVES
    PERFORMANCE FEEDBACK
    REWARD FOR CONTRIBUTION

Chapter 10 ENABLING CHANGE
    THE CHANGE PROCESS
    THE NEED FOR POSITIVE ATTITUDES
    CHANGE STARTS WITH THE INDIVIDUAL
    POINTS OF INTERVENTION
    ENABLING CHANGE

CONCEPTS EXPLORED IN CHAPTER 7

TRANSACTING
  Enabling Behaviour
  Envisioning Achievement
  Establishing Goals and Standards
  Use of Time
ENABLING ROLES
UNDERSTANDING COMMUNICATOR ROLE
  What Influences a Comunication?
  Testing Understanding
  Developing Trust
  Listening and Language
  The Key to Achievement
● *ACHIEVER AND ORCHESTRATOR ROLE*
  Goal Orientation
  Individual and Team Player
  Achieving Synergy
  Self-leadership
● *SOLUTION-SEEKER ROLE*
  Solution-seeking Process
  Unwrapping the Issue
  Testing Reality
  Timeframe
  Creative Solutions
  Choosing a Solution
  Providing Assistance
● *COACH ROLE*
  Improving Performance
  Coaching Process
  Identifying Learner Needs
  Establishing Learning Goals
  Groundrules and Performance Criteria
  Use of Learning Vehicles
● *DEVELOPMENTAL COUNSELLOR ROLE*
  Counselling
  Counselling Environment
  Understanding Expectations
  Groundrules
  Unwrapping the Issue
  Developing Output Objectives
  Counselling Agreement
SUMMARY

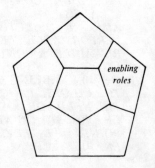

enabling
roles

7 Enabling roles

TRANSACTING

Enabling behaviour

Enabling leadership is displayed by the way enablers handle themselves in situations where others are involved. How they act and behave as they deal with issues and people reflects enabling awareness and philosophy. For example, when handling potential conflict or aggression, the causes are sought and understood as a means of finding a way to resolve the issue satisfactorily. In each situation individuals should feel that they have been involved in a productive event to which they have contributed; feel good about the manner in which the event was facilitated; and their role in the process.

Enabling leaders are aware of the significant differences in outcome which can be achieved through the behaviour displayed during a transaction. They will personally strive to behave in a manner which enhances the possibility of a positive result. We use the term 'behaviour' to describe a situation which represents what one person projects to, and what is perceived by, others. Individuals may not actually speak but will still communicate a great deal to others about their attitudes on an issue.

When people are interacting, 'behaviour' describes:

- what they say
- how it is expressed

- the feelings involved and displayed
- the body language used.

The enabling environment encourages individuals to think before they speak or act, and to be aware of the outcome which may result from the behaviours used in an interaction. Learning 'to engage mind before speaking and acting' is designed to achieve at least two aims. Firstly, to ensure an individual does not say something which disables another individual, and, secondly, to avoid individuals becoming emotionally 'hooked' by the behaviours used by others. Being 'hooked' means responding inappropriately to the behaviour of another individual. Once caught on the 'hook' the possibility of reaching a satisfactory interpersonal solution is considerably reduced.

As enablers transact with individuals, they have a clear aim of communicating effectively by painting specific scenarios which facilitate understanding. They are aware of the potential complexity of the communication process and thus work at keeping the issues as specific and observable as possible. For example, in one four-hour senior management meeting, we observed the following roles and skills being used by the six participants (Figure 7.1).

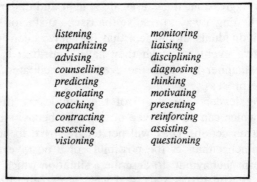

listening	*monitoring*
empathizing	*liaising*
advising	*disciplining*
counselling	*diagnosing*
predicting	*thinking*
negotiating	*motivating*
coaching	*presenting*
contracting	*reinforcing*
assessing	*assisting*
visioning	*questioning*

Figure 7.1   Enabling roles and skills

Understanding the complexity and range of roles and skills used highlights the need for individuals involved in communicating to have a high level of awareness of what is taking place and what they aim to achieve out of the process.

Recognizing the effect behaviour has on a transaction motivates enabling leaders to use their awareness and philosophy to assist them to act in an enabling way. They will be involved in a wide variety of situations which demand a consistent approach using different roles. This chapter focuses on roles used by enablers to achieve win/win results. When observing interactions we identified that enablers:

- have the ability to stimulate individuals to think beyond the present and look into the future
- encourage individuals to draw on the emerging vision and delineate their desires by developing goals and performance standards
- help individuals understand the investment of time and effort required from them to achieve their goals
- behave in a manner which illustrates how to achieve results from being committed, aware and collaborative.

Three components are central to the achievement of effective results. As they form such a significant part of each transaction, we explore them next to build a framework from which enabling roles can be effectively viewed.

Envisioning achievement

Enablers aim to assist people to develop a vision of what they wish to achieve as a result of their investment in an event or activity. Building pictures and obtaining a better awareness of what can be achieved leads to the acceptance of ownership of the emerging scenario. When an individual accepts ownership, the probability is high that he/she will accept responsibility for achieving it. Once a vision has been expressed in terms which individuals understand, they then move on to develop objectives and goals.

Establishing goals and standards

Having a clear picture of what lies ahead can provide two main benefits. Firstly, it provides discipline as there is a requirement to be specific when describing goals using observable/measurable criteria to provide shape and form. Secondly, it helps individuals obtain a better understanding of what they need to do to achieve their goals. Individuals will learn about any 'gap' in attitudes, skills and knowledge which exists between the present and future state they desire.

Once individuals develop their goals, they begin to think about standards of performance to describe what will be different when the goals are achieved. The information developed provides a useful basis for understanding fully what needs to be done and for identifying where and when help is required. Performance standards also help individuals explain the outputs expected from others whom they ask to be involved. Enablers will seek at all times to establish appropriate standards which provide a solid basis for relationships to be effective and thus enhance the process of achieving desired results.

Use of time

Enablers actively encourage individuals to make the most effective use of available time. They raise individuals' awareness of the fact that time is a resource which needs to be managed. In particular, they can learn to manage their time by being clear on the 'how and when' of what they expect to achieve. Individuals also learn that time management is their responsibility and any excuses for having limited time will be viewed by others as saying they have changed priorities in their use of time.

Interacting with enablers provides individuals with insights into what needs to happen and the possible timeframe required. The outcome will involve individuals in planning to ensure that the resources required to achieve the desired goals are drawn together. In some instances an enabler may play a greater part in planning during the early stages. However, there would be an agreed transition of responsibility to the individual as his/her confidence builds.

ENABLING ROLES

This thrust for clarity and understanding by helping individuals envision what could be achieved in the future, if they behave differently, and encouraging individuals to examine their goals to assess the personal investment required, is important to all enablers and is achieved through the use of a variety of enabling roles. Those described in this chapter were observed to be the ones used most consistently by enablers.

The enabling approach is exemplified through its sensitive and responsive approach to encouraging individuals to accept responsibility for achieving results against specific goals. Enablers understand that many individuals are capable of thinking through what they plan to achieve, and setting achievable goals in the process. They also recognize that others need assistance to develop the level of clarity necessary to understand fully the investment required to achieve their goals. The following enabling roles are employed to meet various needs which emerge during transactions between enablers and individuals:

- understanding communicator
- achiever and orchestrator
- solution-seeker
- coach
- developmental counsellor.

The roles are used by enablers to help them and others fulfil the goals they set out to achieve. With reference to our earlier comments on the potential complexity of a communication, the first role is considered by enablers as particularly important as it can make the difference between achievement and non-achievement.

UNDERSTANDING COMMUNICATOR ROLE

An enabler accepts that the primary purpose of a communication is to transmit a message to enable another person to understand its content. To achieve understanding the enabler will think through the following components of a communication:

- is the communication necessary?
- what should it contain?
- what are the receiver's needs?
- how might the receiver perceive the message?
- how should the message be communicated?
- what outputs are expected, and when?

Asking the question 'is the communication necessary?' is an important first step. Evidence from individuals, who after the event regret making certain statements, would certainly support the value of engaging one's mind before acting. It is a useful part of the process to identify the purpose of, and outputs expected from, a communication. As enablers become clear on the expected outcomes, they will turn their attention to understanding the receiver's needs and on how the message can be transmitted to achieve the desired results.

What influences a communication?

Enablers strive to make the message as simple and understandable as possible. This is achieved by thinking of the factors which may influence the effectiveness of the communication. Understanding what the factors are, and how several may be in play at the same time, can help them shape a communication to meet its objectives. Although each transaction will be different, generally one or more of the following need to be considered:

- has the sender's message been developed with the receiver's needs in mind?
- how might the sender feel prior to and during the transaction?
- will the timing of the transaction be managed to enable the environment to be positive?
- what attitudes does the sender hold about the receiver and how will this influence the message and its delivery?
- what might be the receiver's attitude to the sender and the mesage?
- what expectations may the receiver have about the transaction?

As people are different, it is important to strive to understand the particular receiver's needs. Once satisfied that the needs have been identified, individuals should think about appropriate responses they can make to meet them. Preparation is essential at this stage as it can make all the difference to how the communication is received. When satisfied that the needs can be met effectively individuals are ready to conduct the transaction.

Testing understanding

Being aware of the factors that influence situations in which a communication may take place encourages the enabler to use the following process to facilitate the transaction:

- testing to see if the receiver is ready to be involved in the transaction
- setting the scene by explaining the purpose of the transaction
- seeking inputs from receivers as to their understanding of what they expect to cover during the transaction
- obtaining the receiver's commitment to be involved and agreeing ground rules
- transacting the communication and testing to check understanding.

During live transactions enablers will use awareness skills to recognize and interpret signals transmitted by those listening to them. Understanding information received is valuable in enhancing the effectiveness of the transaction. It also provides a framework through which genuine disclosure and feedback can be obtained. Inviting listeners to summarize what they have heard provides feedback on what was understood from the transaction. If the desired message was not understood, it needs to be modified to help the listener.

As the message unfolds, the level of understanding should increase where there is a positive environment which includes feedback, testing and summarizing. When conducted in this environment the enabler is able to modify the message in response to feedback from the listener. Understanding can also be enhanced when the listener perceives a high level of commitment and empathy in the transaction.

Thinking of the other person in terms of his/her needs is essential to communicating. It enables us to think of ways of involving the listener in the process. By inviting the listener to contribute we increase the chances of achieving real understanding. This will be enhanced through a genuine desire to share in a manner which leaves individuals comfortable with the process as they are able to express their thoughts and ideas freely. Listening, hearing and understanding are the key elements in the process of establishing sound relationships. To achieve the desired results when transacting, enablers use their antennae to sense possible blocks to understanding.

Developing trust

Where trust exists, effective channels of communication can be established; thus reducing the danger of distortion from filtering. Enablers are aware that attitudes influence thinking and actions. Therefore, they recognize the benefits to be gained from working to achieve positive conditions within which the transaction can take place. If a person feels threatened, the likely outcome from the transaction could be negative, whereas when the person feels good, the possibility of a positive outcome being realized is considerably enhanced.

An enabler sets about creating a climate of trust designed to induce positive attitudes; thus reducing the potentially damaging effects caused by filtering and interference between the parties involved in a transaction.

Listening and language

Enablers are aware of, and avoid, the following hazards of selective listening:

- only listening to what the other person says until a point of agreement/disagreement is reached; then spending the remaining time thinking about a response whilst the other person continues to talk

- being driven by their own agenda in such a way as to filter what another person says, unless it fits their frame of reference
- using the 'yes . . . but' syndrome in which the receiver appears to listen until the speaker has finished, and then say 'yes . . . but' which is often a prelude to engaging in an evaluative response telling the speaker about how they would act, and what the speaker should do in the situation
- branching out at a tangent from the main point because it happens to provide the listener with an opportunity to talk about a favourite subject
- using language to which the listener cannot relate; often done unconsciously by speakers using words which are normal to them, but are perceived as jargon, or are unintelligible, to the listener.

Active listening is a two-way process: it involves listeners demonstrating to speakers, by the use of appropriate feedback behaviours, their reaction to what they are hearing, and speakers listening and accurately receiving that response. The power of one's own agenda in driving a communication in a specific direction is understood by enablers. They make every effort to understand what others have on their agenda by encouraging them to express what they perceive the issues to be.

As the process continues, enablers seek opportunities to clarify issues where uncertainty exists. When each issue is dealt with in a positive manner an increasing level of understanding is achieved. By listening to what individuals say, they hear the words being used and test their meaning to understand the message better. Therefore, using words which are understood by both parties increases the probability of the message being communicated effectively.

Enablers accept that the primary responsibility for success in communicating rests with the communicator. However they believe that the process is significantly enhanced when it becomes a genuine two-way activity. When enablers understand others, they are better equipped to create a climate which encourages individuals to be involved in a participative process. With some this may take time as their attitudes, influenced by previous experiences, may be negative to the sender and/or message. It may require patience and innovative approaches from an enabler to provide bridges for listeners to cross and feel safe in the process. Once trust and consistency has been built the basis for achieving productive transactions exist.

The key to achievement

Enablers will persist in attempting to create positive relationships which meet the perceived needs and desires of individuals. This helps to ensure that whatever is agreed will be accepted by the parties involved. With a climate of openness and trust it is possible to achieve a high level of understanding from all transactions. Individuals are motivated to listen to, and understand, the message being communicated and how it affects them. If action is required, they want to fully understand the contribution expected from them.

Clarity in communications provides confidence in moving forward to achieve results. We can realize the significant benefits, which come from an investment in developing our ability to communicate effectively. Enabling leadership demands a high standard of performance when communicating as enablers recognize it holds the key to understanding and eventual achievement.

ACHIEVER AND ORCHESTRATOR ROLE

Enabling leaders have an achievement orientation. They are motivated to clarify what is to be accomplished in every situation in which they are involved. From this clarity they understand the contribution they can make and how it fits with the overall expectations of the group or organization. Being able to understand their contribution, and compare it with the outcomes expected, provides them with an awareness of what needs to be done. It also enables them to develop an awareness of the contribution to be made by others involved in the process.

Being able to interpret and understand situations provides enablers with insights into how to construct relationships which enable organizational outputs to be achieved. This starts with enablers understanding their own needs and the contribution required to achieve the result from their involvement. Through analysis and understanding of self and other team members, enablers work towards creating an environment of achievement. Within such an environment the enabler will seek opportunities for everyone to contribute towards the overall goals. This can be accomplished by developing a clear understanding of what is to be achieved and providing a framework within which individuals can play their part.

Goal orientation

Such a framework would be constructed using the following key elements:

- identifying the specific goals to be accomplished
- agreeing tasks and roles with each member of the team in relation to the contribution they wish to make
- understanding what is expected from each individual and/or team
- developing performance standards which enables progress to be identified and monitored
- understanding of what recognition and benefits will be obtained from successful accomplishment of the goals.

Individuals would be involved in the process of obtaining a clear picture of what was to be achieved, when, and what benefits would be available. Their contribution is made within a framework established through discussion and consistent with agreed objectives. Individuals who work with enablers expect that what they say will be done. Individuals can depend on enablers as their behaviour and actions are congruent with what they think, say and do.

Individual and team player

There are times when an organization requires enablers to make their contribution as individuals and other times as members of a team. At all times they are able to make their contribution in a functional manner designed to help the organization progress towards it goals. If an individual contribution is required, it is done in a way which meets the expectations of the organization. When the contribution is made as part of a team, enablers perform effectively as team players. Being aware of the effect that they have on a team, and how this influences the team achievement, is fundamental to enablers.

Crucial to an enabler's effectiveness is a willingness to give and receive feedback on behaviour and performance. This can be of positive benefit to individuals and enablers when done within an enabling environment. It provides guidance on how well the team is performing as measured against performance targets. Adverse variations to team or individual member performance can be discussed to agree what can be done to correct the situation. When performance is on or above target, enablers ensure that the facts are fed back to the team as this can provide powerful positive reinforcement and motivation.

Working to establish and improve the open, sharing, caring and collaborative environment (described in Chapters 8 and 9) is an enabler's primary objective. Enablers know that in such a dynamic and positive environment all members of the team feel able and committed to make their contribution.

Achieving synergy

A significant outcome from a sound team environment is a level of performance greater than the sum of the team members involved. Synergy can be achieved when team members:

- identify with the organization's goals
- understand the contribution they can make
- recognize the importance of relating effectively with others
- accept responsibility for managing their resources
- recognize the needs which others have
- are willing and committed to make an agreed contribution
- are accountable for their actions.

Synergy can be achieved when individuals make their contributions in a manner designed to add value to the organization. When individuals are respected, they are more inclined to be responsible in what they say and do.

Involvement and real participation in decision making provides components of an environment which encourages individuals to act in a manner congruent with organizational aims. They will become proactive and make their contribution with the minimum need for supervision, and with feedback provided by team members. It is from within this positive type of environment that self and shared leadership emerges.

Self-leadership

Enabling leadership is about creating environments through which every member of a team is energized to achieve the highest level of performance to fulfil agreed goals. As individuals learn to collaborate to achieve individual and organizational goals, they find that their contribution brings fulfilment and growth. Their confidence in being able to achieve grows and, at the same time, it encourages the growth of self-leadership.

Self-leadership describes a state of individual competence which makes individuals feel able and confident to assume leadership when making their contribution. They will express their leadership in many different ways designed to move the team towards achieving its goals. On occasions this will involve leading from the front in an assertive manner and at other times leading by allowing others to lead. The process allows individuals to try their hand at assuming a leadership role and gain confidence through the experience. However, it should be understood that the behaviours used will be congruent withthe enabling philosophy. The environment encourages leadership to be shared as an effective process for enabling individuals to add their knowledge and skills to enhance the team's performance.

Enabling leadership is therefore about empowering individuals to feel able to make a significant contribution. This will be commensurate with their level of ability, motivation, commitment and potential to develop. When individuals recognize their potential to grow and develop, they are motivated to acquire new skills to enhance their ability to contribute and receive appropriate recognition.

The environment will be one which exhibits excitement, fun, enjoyment, energy, purpose and sense of achievement. It also recognizes the whole person and will take account of the social, mental, physical and spiritual needs of those involved. As individuals are recognized to have different needs, enablers will encourage their individuality to be expressed within a framework congruent with achieving organizational goals.

Individuals are expected to be accountable for their actions and to show respect for others as they contribute towards achieving the organizational goals. They 'know' what is expected and are given discretion to draw from their experience to fulfil their agreed contribution. Enablers aim to involve individuals in the process of 'knowing' where the organization is going to enable them to add value in all that they do.

Although enablers predominantly aim towards achievement of the organization's goals, they are aware that these goals must include recognition of the potential of individuals. This recognition and commitment to individual and team growth, within an open collaborative framework, provides a powerful basis for individuals to give of their best: because they identify with the goals, with the people and with the organization in such a way that the benefits derived are win/win.

SOLUTION-SEEKER ROLE

In periods of rapid change individuals are confronted with an increasing number of situations which require decisions to be made. Enabling leaders recognize a tendency for some individuals to avoid making decisions because of the level of risk and degree of ambiguity surrounding a particular issue. Individuals will, therefore, react differently when faced with a difficult issue which requires their attention to resolve. The outcome is dependent on how they view the issue and the attitude they adopt. We describe two scenarios which illustrate what can happen.

If a particular issue is viewed as a problem and the analysis puts a great deal of emphasis on the difficulty of resolving the problem the chances are individuals will revert to one of the following responses:

- avoid making a decision because there is insufficient information available
- procrastinate
- leave the problem alone in the belief it will go away
- pass the problem to someone else
- rationalize and thus remove the problem
- state all the difficulties to block exploration of potential solutions.

Alternatively, if the issue is viewed as an opportunity to be solved and the focus is one of solution-seeking, the response from individuals may be

- open minds to explore the issue
- analysis of the issue to obtain as many 'facts' as possible
- obtain clarity on what outcomes are expected or desired by testing facts and assumptions
- look for options which offer appropriate solutions
- involve people in the solution to gain commitment and ownership.

Developing a solution-seeking focus means identifying a range of options to solve particular issues. Identifying options and thinking through the outcomes from each solution, can provide better possibilities for solving a particular issue. This can be facilitated through the use of a solution-seeking process which provides a framework for individuals to shape the issue and thus provide a springboard for identifying solutions.

Solution-seeking process

We describe a dynamic process, comprising a number of elements, which provides a sound framework for finding solutions. Although the steps are listed in a sequential manner, in practice they are used in a flexible way dependent on the needs of individuals and the issue. The reality of dealing with most issues is that, as we examine and analyse them, information and perceptions become available which require us on occasions to go back to the drawing board. Therefore the following elements should be viewed as parts of a dynamic process:

- raise awareness of the issue through exploration and unwrapping of the factors involved
- identify causes of problem/opportunity and make a statement which defines the issues
- test realities by exploring expectations, bias, prejudice and other values which filter understanding of the information available
- identify the needs, wishes, desires associated with the issue
- timeframe
- use creativity in generating solutions
- choose solution which offers the best route to achieving the desired outcome
- prepare a map of the steps required to translate the solution into reality
- marshal the resources required to achieve the desired outcome
- assess performance and monitor progress to identify opportunities to modify and upgrade solutions.

Unwrapping the issue

At the early stages of the process considerable emphasis is given to analysing the issue to obtain clarity around what actually exists and what needs to be done to modify the situation. This is important as considerable difficulty can be experienced in fully understanding the real cause of a particular problem or why an opportunity exists.

There is a tendency for some individuals to be over optimistic/pessimistic in the way they view a particular issue. They may become either excited about the possibilities perceived in the opportunity or depressed by the difficulties thrown up by the problem. An enabler encourages the individual to 'step out' of the issue and attempt to explore it from a detached and objective position.

An outcome from the analysis stage is an expression (statement) of the problem/opportunity in terms which enables individuals to produce a map of reality of the situation. An enabler will encourage individuals to describe their expectations and attitudes to the issue as a means of understanding any negative filters which need to be included in the reality mapping process.

Testing reality

Testing reality is the part of the process which explores just how realistic individual expectations are and their motivation for taking action to modify a situation. Within each map of reality the modifications which are perceived necessary would be examined in the light of the following three levels:

- needs
- wishes
- dreams.

Needs

The first level, 'need', would be identified as a specific measurable and observable requirement the individual had for making a particular decision. For example, if the individual wished to purchase a new car and had an amount of money available which could not be exceeded, this would be identified as a 'need' to be fulfilled. In many instances the ability to identify 'needs' can be a powerful means of understanding the parts that, if not met, will not fulfil the desired objective.

Wishes

With the second level, 'wishes', an individual has a higher level of discretion in finding a solution. To illustrate 'wishes' let us return to the car purchase example. An individual may wish to purchase a red car with four doors. If a blue car which meets the financial need is found and it has four doors, it could be a satisfactory solution. However if red is the only acceptable colour this factor would move from a 'wish' to a 'need' and become more significant in the decision-making process.

Dreams

The third level, 'dreams', refers to an over-optimistic impression held by individuals in which they believe there is nothing to stop them achieving a particular objective. However, on closer examination, they discover there is limited evidence to support their dream being fulfilled. This is not to deny the value of encouraging people to envision which might sometimes relate to the dream state. The major difference will be in an individual's understanding of the process. The need is to understand visioning as a technique for painting scenarios which, after processing, can lead to effective solutions, as against 'wishful thinking' associated with a dream state.

Timeframe

Another factor which plays an important part in the process is the question of time. With some issues the whole process from identification, unwrapping, goal-setting through to completion may take minutes. Whereas in other situations, it may take weeks, months or even years to be achieved. The shorter the timeframe, the more dynamic the process will be in handling feedback on progress towards achievement.

Enablers will be aware of the passage of time and how some individuals are easily disillusioned if the desired outcome is not realized quickly. It is therefore vital to develop performance standards, with agreed timeframes, to provide individuals with a framework to assess their performance. Such a framework can be developed by encouraging individuals to establish their goals in timeframes which are described as short-, medium- and long-term. This can provide an understandable framework and motivation as some of the short-term goals can cover days rather than weeks. Progress towards achievement of a medium-term goal can then be more readily observed. Being able to see the big picture, as represented by the long-term goals, will be enhanced by a process which paints in the detail of how to get there. The framework does not guarantee that individuals may not become demotivated. However, it does help individuals obtain a picture of the time they may need to achieve a goal. In addition, it provides a vehicle for assessing progress and getting feedback to explore where they are at a particular point in time.

Creative solutions

An enabler's response to the ambiguity and uncertainty which surrounds situations and issues is to approach solutions with creative thinking. We think of creative thinking as an individual's ability to bring into being, or to form through force of imagination, unique solutions to a particular issue.

Being able to imagine potential solutions will require individuals to 'let go' of their logical and sequential thinking. A technique used to do this is termed 'visioning'. It uses a process of guided imagery to encourage individuals to let go of the present. Guided imagery is facilitated through the use of brainstorming, depicting and scenario painting. All are designed to encourage individuals to use the intuitive, creative and visual parts of their brain. The objective of visioning is to provide a process which encourages individuals to use their whole brain to arrive at original solutions to the issue under review.

Through this form of examination new information may become available which allows individuals to modify the solution or, alternatively, their expectation and subsequently develop different approaches.

Choosing a solution

Once a range of solutions with their perceived outcomes has been identified, the next step is to arrive at a decision on a solution which best meets the individual's needs. An advantage of having a range of options available comes from a recognition that one particular solution may meet a short-term need whereas a combination of several solutions may meet longer-term needs. At all times the enabler encourages individuals to perceive what it would be like when the solution has been accomplished. The sharper the picture of what the outcome will feel, sound and look like, the more likely a decision on a particular solution will be made. This part of the process provides a strong incentive for individuals to own the final solution. And through ownership comes the motivation to achieve.

Providing assistance

Enablers provide encouragement to individuals to work towards implementing their chosen solution. In most instances motivation is linked to an individual's understanding of what is involved coupled with confidence in believing that it can be achieved. Therefore, the early work done in obtaining clarity about the issue, and in generating solutions based on an agreed map of reality, can provide a sound foundation on which an individual will work towards fulfilment of the solution. The enabler's aim is continually to reinforce the positive outcomes of the work being done by the individual as a means of building confidence and of reducing dependency.

A solution-seeking environment is one which encourages open disclosure and feedback between the individual and enabler. This provides an excellent opportunity for issues to be explored in an effective manner designed to produce realizable solutions. Within the environment there is the freedom to succeed and/or fail as a means of gaining relevant experience on which individuals can grow. This freedom also provides a powerful incentive for individuals to monitor and diagnose progress towards achieving a particular solution. As information is gleaned which may have an impact on the application of the solution, appropriate action can be taken to modify the solution or outcome to suit a new set of circumstances.

COACH ROLE

One of the central components of an enabling philosophy is the genuine desire to empower. Although this extends to many aspects of a relationship, it relates, in particular, to the transfer of knowledge, skill and techniques to others. Enablers are committed to assist individuals achieve their goals. All assistance would be consistent with the enabling philosophy of encouraging individuals to be self-managed learners.

Many individuals recognize the value of having an ability to work towards acquiring new knowledge and skills in an independent manner. They also see there is still considerable scope in seeking assistance from people who have acquired the skills. However, they understand that it is not just a simple transfer 'by telling'. Rather, it is a genuine sharing by the parties involved. An exciting outcome of such a sharing relationship is the realization that learning is a two-way process.

Coaching provides enablers with opportunities to assist individuals improve their performance. There will be a variety of reasons for individuals wishing to acquire additional knowledge and skills. To illustrate the enabling approach to coaching we briefly describe the following components:

- improving performance
- coaching process
- identifying learning needs
- establishing learning goals
- commitment to learn.

Improving performance

In many business situations the rate of change brought about by technology and fluctuating markets means that many individuals are being asked to adapt their skills to meet different administrative and operational needs. Enabling leadership seeks ways to keep individuals equipped to ensure they maintain the organization's effectiveness and competitive advantage. One positive approach is to create an environment which motivates individuals to be proactive learners. Individuals in the organization who understand and effectively apply the skills and knowledge required in the change situation can be used as coaches. Given their willingness, and an understanding of how to transfer learning, they can provide others with the appropriate skills and knowledge.

Learning transfer can be extremely effective if it is done through an enabling coaching process. The role of coach is to facilitate the acquisition of skills, knowledge, techniques, attitudes and behaviours appropriate to the requirements of a particular job, task or activity. The key to effective transfer of learning is in the coaching relationship and the process used.

Coaching process

The enabler's aim is to establish a positive relationship which provides the learner with support, guidance and confidence to manage his/her learning. To achieve the right type of environment and climate of learning, the following elements of the coaching process would be constructed to meet the needs of the coaching relationship:

- identification of learning need
- development of clearly expressed goals in measurable/observable terms
- establishment of ground rules which enable the parties to make the best use of time and talent
- agreement on performance criteria which can be used to assess progress against agreed timeframes
- use of learning vehicles which enable learning transfer to be achieved in an empowering manner.

Working together, an individual and enabler can achieve a clear understanding of what is expected from a coaching relationship. This enables both parties to travel in the same direction designed to achieve the identified outputs.

Identifying learning needs

Being aware of what needs to be learned is the first essential step in the coaching process. An individual must be able to obtain a clear picture of what he or she aims to achieve from a coaching relationship. As stated earlier, it is very important to obtain a clear picture of what will be different at the end of the process. Enablers will work with individuals to encourage them to explore the reasons for wanting to learn and what they expect to achieve from the acquisition of new learning. They will be encouraged to think in specific terms to focus on how much of the learning process will be within their control.

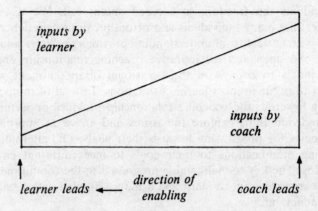

Figure 7.2 Learner/coach continuum

Figure 7.2 illustrates the different degrees of learning responsibility held by the coach and learner. The objective will be to see the transfer of responsibility for learning moving from the coach to the learner in an effective manner. This should be achieved as smoothly as possible whilst recognizing that there will be occasions when the learner, having acquired certain standards, will need to re-engage with a coach to break new ground. However, the main thrust should still be on the learner managing the learning. One way of ensuring this is done would be through the development of clear goals which identify the main outputs from the learning process.

Establishing learning goals

Identifying learning goals and expressing them in observable/measurable terms provides individuals with an opportunity to think about how they will be achieved. As they examine each of the learning goals they will be able to identify the parts they will be able to manage themselves because of their existing knowledge and experience. The enabler will be aware of the need to coach an individual to set goals which provide sufficient stimulus and challenge without being too ambitious or unrealistic.

A sound coaching relationship provides a climate which allows individuals the freedom to succeed and/or fail. We discussed earlier that many individuals learn from previous experience and gain a great deal from understanding previous successes and failures. An open and collaborative coaching relationship enables individuals to cope with the occasional disappointment which tends to occur in most learning situations. Instead of motivation being lowered, the coaching relationship provides opportunities for individuals to explore the issues and arrive at appropriate strategies for progressing towards their goals. Or, alternatively, making modifications to their goals to meet different circumstances. The key to maintaining progress is in the commitment of the learner to want to learn and achieve, coupled with flexibility and adaptability.

Groundrules and performance criteria

The next stage in the process establishes a framework to enable the coach and learner to build a coaching relationship and monitor its effectiveness. They work together to establish a set of groundrules within which the coaching relationship will operate. The enabling coach strives, during the process of establishing groundrules, to encourage individuals to identify how they will manage the learning process. This takes account of existing confidence and competence of individuals to accomplish successfully what they set out to achieve.

Groundrules should help individuals develop productive relationships with their coach. They cover each stage of the process and provide indicators which tell the parties how well progress is being maintained.

Use of learning vehicles

We discussed in Chapter 6 the importance of learning styles. Enablers, armed with awareness of learning styles, can work with learners to discover appropriate vehicles to assist learning. For example, a highly participative event would suit some learners as it involves a 'hands on' experience which would suit their learning style, whereas for other learners this would not meet their need for careful explanations of what is required before tackling a task. Selecting the correct learning vehicle is important for many reasons associated with motivating individuals to learn and achieve.

Advancements in learning technology now allow organizations and individuals a wide range of choice. They can choose from highly structured learning events to ones which are very flexible, open-ended and learner-managed. The key to selection lies in awareness of what needs to be learned, how quickly, and the learning preferences of the individual. From this the choice of learning vehicle should be a relatively simple task. For example, to provide development opportunities in an organization the use of multidisciplinary project/task groups have been effective as they provide a highly focused and relatively short-term exposure to real organizational issues.

The coaching process is effective when it operates as an empowering process. The greater clarity the learner has about what he or she expects to accomplish through a coaching relationship, the higher the probability of it being accomplished. There is a significant responsibility placed on the coach to be aware of the inherent danger of dependency being established in a relationship. This is caused by the coach being motivated by ego strokes received from being the 'master', coupled with potential immaturity, uncertainty and lack of confidence in the learner. Enablers are aware of this danger and ensure through their behaviour that the focus of the learning process is on building confidence and competence in the learner. Ways by which this can be achieved are discussed in Chapter 6.

DEVELOPMENTAL COUNSELLOR ROLE

We use the term 'developmental counselling' to describe a process which:

- is a relationship of equals, designed to empower
- encourages an individual to learn how to analyse and understand the relevant factors involved in the issue under review
- develops an individual's skills to seek solutions which meet

his/her perceived needs thus ensuring ownership and commitment to working out the solutions
- establishes objectives and goals for achieving the solution to meet the desired outcome
- provides a framework of support which encourages individuals to put solutions into action with the minimum of personal dependency on others
- establishes standards and measurement criteria which allow progress to be monitored by the individual.

Counselling

There will be situations in which individuals find it difficult to see clearly what action should be taken to deal with a problem or opportunity. Where a climate of trust and positive support is present, they are encouraged to explore the issues with an enabler. Each party to the discussion will establish their roles and responsibilities to ensure there is no doubt with whom responsibility for subsequent action lies. The individual works to find and then implement suitable solutions. The role of the enabling counsellor in the process is to:

- help create a positive climate in which they can work together
- develop a relationship in which the individual does not feel subordinated
- act as a catalyst and reflector in feeding back perceptions on the information developed by the individual
- encourage the individual to explore the issues and develop solutions
- help the individual visualize the outcomes expected
- encourage the efforts of the individual in attempting to solve the issue, thus reinforcing the value of the freedom to succeed or fail.

A trusting relationship provides a foundation on which the enabler can confront an individual in a positive manner to provide feedback. When carried out positively, it provides individuals with confidence to seek honest feedback on the effectiveness of the diagnostic process and their ability to unwrap the issues.

It is a dynamic process which establishes a developmental framework for an individual to work through an issue to arrive at a suitable solution. The environment created by the enabler allows the individual freedom to explore the issues in a creative manner. Being able to explore and unwrap the issues to understand fully what needs to be done, and why, provides a basis of confidence for an individual to achieve the solution.

Counselling environment

Placed high on the enabler's agenda is the creation of an environment which encourages individuals to feel able to express thoughts and feelings freely about an opportunity/problem. The aim is to develop a relationship which encourages them to explore the issues, with confidence, in a non-threatening climate. The main question is how to create an appropriate environment, recognizing that different people have different needs.

Expressing belief in equality, being accepting and non-judgemental and exploring the fact that a solution cannot be found without an individual's fullest participation, can establish a basis for building confidence in the process. An enabler has the patience to continue building the relationship to enable individuals gain confidence in the process.

The environment is established by the enabler's behaviour, coupled with those physical characteristics which assists individuals to feel relatively safe and relaxed. Working to achieve such positive relationships with individuals is a sound investment as it provides opportunities for them to explore issues in an empowered way.

Understanding expectations

It is essential for an enabler to gain a clear understanding with the individual on what are the expected roles and outcomes. This step can provide a sound framework for the relationship to function with the minimum of misunderstanding. Enablers recognize the positive advantages to be gained from encouraging individuals develop a sharp awareness of what will be achieved from the counselling process. The aim is one of clarifying, at an early stage, what an individual has in his/her mind about what may be achieved from developmental counselling.

Groundrules

Establishing a set of groundrules provides an opportunity for the parties involved to clarify expectations, roles and develop a framework within which the counselling process can be managed. Increasing the arena of understanding, will maximize the chances of the counselling intervention being effective in meeting an individual's needs. The primary outcome from this part of the process should be a clear understanding of how counselling will be conducted and the leadership required by the individual to ensure it functions to meet his/her needs. Once agreement has been reached, the process can then move forward to deal with the 'why' element of the counselling intervention. Both parties will be aware that circumstances can change and will learn to modify the ground rules to take account of these differences.

Analysing the issue

Enablers can assist in the analysing process by asking questions. These will be designed to enable the individual to think clearly about the issue. Learning to express thoughts and ideas freely without being judged can provide a real stimulus to delve into the issue. Active listening coupled with open-ended questions, rephrasing and summarizing can help the individual put shape to the issue.

Working through this part of the process with sensitivity and understanding should enable the individual to be in possession of sufficient information, and clarity about what it means, to decide to continue the counselling process. Once the individual has made this decision, the next step is to think about the outputs from the investment. By this time the individual should clearly understand and own the issue, and feel responsible for its eventual resolution.

The enabler will encourage an individual to obtain a focus on what is expected. This will usually start with a broad brush statement which may range from specific to rather vague scenarios. The process allows the individual to clarify and build the scenario in such a way that it becomes understandable and achievable.

Developing output objectives

Obtaining a description of output objectives in terms which are observable and/or measurable means that performance towards them can be understood and monitored. To illustrate the point here is an example drawn from a recent counselling situation:

- Initial statement of counselling goal 'I want to be able to talk to groups of people without feeling anxious and becoming tongue tied'
- After initial counselling the statement was reshaped to say 'I will be able to make a 15-minute presentation on the "Summer Project" to groups of my colleagues in six weeks' time. I will prepare the presentation and use visual aids to support the words (and to give me time to think). I will work at being relaxed by practising deep and steady breathing.'

The statement continued with several behavioural performance standards being expressed which represented how the individual envisioned the way he would make the presentation. Time spent obtaining an understandable picture of what an individual expects to achieve is well worth the effort. As the vision starts to be realized, it can provide increasing levels of motivation to drive the person forward.

Counselling agreement

In some instances the parties like to formalize their roles/inputs and a counselling agreement can be devised to fulfil this need. The agreement brings together the goals, timeframe, performance standards and ground rules established by an individual. Where a contribution from others is required to assist the learning process, their role and part in the process is identified and recorded. Outcomes are expressed in a language which describes what difference in behaviour and performance will be achieved. All parties to the agreement sign off to show this interest and commitment to the process and the individual. Some individuals find that a counselling agreement provides an effective vehicle for enhancing commitment and subsequent action.

The agreement is expressed in clear and understandable language with the minimum of formality. The term 'agreement' is used to describe a level of commitment to the process. In other instances these areas are noted in a less formal manner. The important point is to achieve understanding, agreement and commitment from all involved.

SUMMARY

Enablers adopt particular roles to help all individuals involved in an organizational activity to achieve the desired outcomes. Being able to understand what exists in each relationship as it takes place, coupled with awareness of the environment, provides them with the ability to 'sense' which role or roles are needed. The measure of success comes from individuals motivating themselves to make their contribution in a manner which adds value. As we explore enabling organizations and enabling contribution in Chapters 8 and 9, the key significance of enabling roles will be further illustrated and reinforced.

CONCEPTS EXPLORED IN CHAPTER 8

AN ENABLING ORGANIZATION
  Dynamic and Proactive
  Valuing Contribution
  Enabling Environment
  Creating an Enabling Organization
ORGANIZATIONAL MISSION
ORGANIZATIONAL CULTURE
  Managing Change Through Culture
  How Culture is Created
  Linking Values to the Mission
SHARED VALUES
  Culture and Values
  Living the Values
  Owning the Values
  Setting Relevant Norms/Standards
  Historical Culture
  Changing Values
DEVELOPING INDIVIDUALS AND TEAMS
  Encouraging Individual Growth
  Openness and Trust
  Belief in People and Their Capability
  Provides Team-building Opportunities
  Multidisciplinary Development
  Focus on Outputs and Accountability

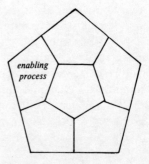

enabling process

8 Enabling process (1) – enabling organization

AN ENABLING ORGANIZATION

Dynamic and proactive

Being involved in an enabling organization is an exciting and fulfilling activity as if offers individuals the opportunity to be part of a purposeful activity to which they can make a contribution and receive appropriate rewards for their efforts. If we explore what makes such an organization 'tick', we could identify a set of policies and procedures which enable the organization's resources to be used effectively to achieve its objectives. However, many organizations have policies and procedures which have become static, mechanistic and no longer able to respond to the dynamic needs placed on them. This awareness is slowly dawning on an increasing number of organizations as they realize that, to be competitive in the late 1980s and onwards in a rapidly changing world, they require quite different forms of organization. Being able to develop new types of organization to meet specific needs and demands will require a proactive process. We need to understand organizations to enable us to identify where and when to make strategic and tactical interventions. This is why the term culture is increasingly being used to describe a process of understanding the dynamic nature of organizations.

Enabling leadership applies to the development of enabling processes which allow individuals to be effective in whatever activity they are engaged to perform. We use the term enabling process to describe an organization's culture, and what it does to create and maintain an environment which encourages its people to be actively involved and committed to making a genuine contribution to its success. To take this idea further, we consider that an organization whose people resources achieve effective results tends to be an enabling organization. This can be defined as:

an enabling organization is one which has a clearly stated mission and shared values which defines its culture. The culture values people and produces an environment which encourages individuals to:

- be involved in developing shared goals
- work individually and in teams to achieve the goals
- accept leadership positions as situations require
- respect each other and feel good about themselves
- be willing to contribute more if it helps colleagues and the organization
- look for better ways to perform tasks and assignments.

When an organization achieves the blending of its characteristics into a well-understood culture it has attained a significant stage in its own development. It is also likely to have a significant number of individuals operating as enablers facilitating the enabling process. As their actions and behaviour will be congruent with the culture they will encourage people to feel a part of something special. We shall now explore what enablers can do in an organization to achieve the outputs expressed for an enabling organization.

Valuing contribution

An enabling organization values people and this forms a significant part of its culture. Value is built on an awareness and understanding of the respect which each individual has for others as displayed within the organization. This naturally influences the way individuals deal with each other and is reflected in a positive climate for personal growth. It is interesting to note that an increasing number of organizations are now working to build their products and services.

Enablers work at creating sound relationships consistent with the high respect they feel for individuals. They recognize the simple truth that when individuals feel good about themselves the more able and willing they are to make an effective contribution to an organization. And, experience shows that people operate more effectively when they have a clear understanding of what contribution they can make.

They also feel good when they understand and believe in the direction the organization is taking. Being aware of its direction provides them with a degree of certainty of what they need to do to meet the organization's goals.

Enabling environment

Enabling leadership therefore involves working in organizations to develop environments within which people are actively involved in achieving its goals – because they have a part to play in shaping them. They also relate to the organization's mission and understand how it provides a focus to their efforts in achieving results. This produces an equation in which the sum of the collective effort contributed is greater than the sum of the individual contributions. When this is achieved, we are describing the realization of synergy within the organization. People feel able to make a more selfless contribution as the environment provides them with the opportunity to be actively involved in decision making, particularly with decisions which affect them.

Enablers strive to create a working framework of shared values with clear goal orientation to which individuals can relate their own special contribution. We therefore promote the significance of developing an environment which enables individuals to want to make a genuine contribution as a means of adding value to the organization, and thus to everyone involved.

Creating an enabling organization

Enablers will be involved in seeking ways by which an enabling process can be created within an organization. They will actively seek other enablers to form enabling networks to provide a sound base on which to construct enabling processes. To understand what enablers do to develop the architecture of an enabling organization, we explore the following components:

● organizational mission
● culture
● shared values
● developing individuals and teams.

Although each enabling organization may be different, there are sufficient factors identified to provide a clear picture of what can be done to achieve and maintain effectiveness. The following ideas will provide key indicators to enable us to chart a route to create enabling organizations. An effective way of providing this clarity is through the development of a mission statement which describes why the organization exists and what makes it different from others.

ORGANIZATIONAL MISSION

A mission statement provides key direction to all individuals involved in an organization. It provides a framework within which they can relate their own contribution to the organization's goals. The mission also provides decision makers with a template to test their thinking process and assist decision making which keeps the organization effectively positioned in the marketplace.

An increasing number of organizations have or are developing mission statements. This reflects the value such a statement has as a vehicle to describe what an organization is in existence to achieve. Mission statements are expressed in many different forms and are sometimes described as a credo or philosophy. It is important to choose a description which enables people involved in an organization to relate to its message. The term mission now has wide corporate acceptance as it can encompass the dynamic vision of what an organization is all about.

To illustrate the value of a mission statement we have culled the following example from a number of statements of which we have personal experience:

> XYZ is committed to providing quality products and services which meet customers' needs and provide them with value for money. We shall work in an open, collaborative and innovative manner to enable us to produce and deliver our products and services in an effective and courteous way.

The messages contained in the mission statement can be interpreted as saying:

- the company will supply products and services to agreed quality standards
- the products and services will be designed to meet customers' needs
- customers will receive value for money
- the products and services will be produced and delivered in effective and courteous ways
- team working will be encouraged through openness and collaboration
- innovation will be encouraged in all that people do to add value to the products and services.

The mission is designed to provide clear direction for all members of the organization and to assist them understand the framework within which their organization sets its goals. It sets out in understandable form how the organization expects its members to contribute to enable it to achieve its goals.

The mission statement will have maximum impact when it is developed through a participative process which allows all organizational members to contribute. As the mission is shaped through this process, it provides every individual with the opportunity to understand what it means. Individuals can then choose to be involved in the organization as they know what is expected from them. Understanding what the mission means is a vital part of the enabling process as, once accepted, it becomes an internalized part of an individual's belief system.

ORGANIZATIONAL CULTURE

Culture can be defined as a set of shared values within an organization to which people can identify and contribute. Our research demonstrates that every organization has at least one main culture in existence with other subcultures representing divisions, departments, sections and groups. Culture can be recognized by the behaviours displayed and activities carried out within an organization as it strives to achieve its goals. The behaviours and activities can be either positive or negative depending on how the organization rewards and punishes what people do in the performance of their jobs.

To illustrate the point we describe the attitudes which were displayed in one outlet of a well-known icecream chain over a period of two weeks. The organization clearly promotes customer service through its quality product and innovative service. On numerous occasions we observed customer needs being met in an effective manner with occasional innovation. The result was high customer satisfaction and considerable brand loyalty in one area which hosted three other competing outlets in close proximity. The shop was busy and full of activity most of the time. However, when one of the two supervisors was present the whole atmosphere changed. When customers asked for combinations which they had become accustomed to receive they were abruptly told that their request was not possible. In addition, the supervisor asked to be told which members of staff had fulfilled the requests so that he could reprimand them. His attitude caused initial puzzlement then hostility from customers, resulting in lost sales and the shop becoming quite deserted during the supervisor's shift. The difference was dramatic and was attributable entirely to the behaviours displayed. It should also be noted that the practices used by the staff were in no way deviant but sound examples of real customer service.

Here is one of the most powerful aspects of culture when the agreed values are understood and accepted. We find that the existence of a shared mission supported by an appropriate culture will generally reduce incidences of such ineffective behaviour in an organization. As the values are understood and shared, negative behaviour is clearly perceived to be deviant in terms of the mission. Individuals or groups who deviate, whether unwittingly or not, can be identified and made aware of the potentially damaging effect of their actions. Assistance is provided through a positive counselling process to enable individuals to become aware of the effect of their actions and to realize the adverse impact of their behaviour. If no change takes place, the culture encourages the individual to choose whether to stay or leave the organization. The culture supports all types of individual behaviour as long as it is congruent with the mission.

Managing change through culture

Being aware of its culture can provide an organization with a powerful technique for effecting change to produce beneficial results for all involved. This enables an organization to understand which parts of its culture need to be altered to facilitate change. Culture needs to be examined with as much detail as would be invested in, say, the production of a new car, perfume or process plant. And to achieve effective outcomes requires organizations to shape their culture with as much care as they apply to a product or an investment. We perceive that the development of a sound culture provides the following benefits to an organization:

- helps people to relate to the organization as they learn to understand the shared values and behaviours.
- provides a framework of symbols, language and meaning which enables individuals to understand the organization and what it is about
- lets people express their own individuality within well-understood parameters. If the culture changes to a point where it conflicts with the personal values of an individual, the person must choose between trying to influence and reshape the values and leaving.
- individuals learn to internalize the process and procedures used in a wide range of situations. This enables them to under-

stand how to respond positively to whatever they confront in the execution of their duties from the usual to the bizarre.

The enabling process can build a set of shared values which provides individuals with respect and a sense of worth which allows them to feel an integral part of the organization. It is therefore important to understand how such a culture can be constructed.

How culture is created

As we examine an organization and identify its shared values, we may be able to understand what makes it function, particularly from the people perspective. In most cases the culture of an organization is initially established by the person or persons who created it, with reshaping being done by the current leadership. Culture is therefore shaped by the way leaders act and behave in setting and meeting the organization's objectives. This establishes the values which set standards of behaviour and performance outputs required.

For example, if the individuals leading an organization express a desire for quality in all that the organization does, and their behaviour in working to achieve the standard of quality is congruent, there is a high probability that the quality standards will be achieved. These quality standards will be personally inter-nalized thus reinforcing the culture and ensuring that new recruits who join the organization will understand and accept this value and work to maintain the standards.

Most organizations seek to provide a sense of direction to enable their people to channel their energies into fulfilling the organization's objectives. The sharper the direction coupled with involvement in shaping its objectives, can provide people with a sense of purpose and commitment to work to achieve. This is why we consider a mission provides direction and focus on the future to which people can relate.

The mission statement sets the scene and expresses the organiz-ation's purpose in existing. Although establishing a mission is a vital step in providing direction, as much care is required in thinking through the values which support it. Our definition of a value may help establish a benchmark for subsequent use:

a value is an internalized belief system which influences the attitudes formed by an individual to an internal and/or external stimulus. The value is perceived by others through the actions and behaviours displayed by the individual.

For example, when an individual respects others and lives by the value of courtesy, the behaviours used in situations will display courtesy to others. This can be achieved in a variety of ways when the individual has internalized the value and has the skills to cope with a diverse range of behaviours from others.

We stated earlier that an organization's culture comprises the values which are shared by its members. Achieving a sharing of values is vital to enable individuals to understand how they are expected to operate to fulfil the mission. However, we find this is the state to which organizations fail to give sufficient emphasis and attention. Lack of follow-through arises because of the knowing/doing syndrome.

We have observed individuals expressing support for organizational values because they intellectually believed in them. Yet the behaviours they subsequently displayed within the organization were not congruent with their values. These individuals 'knew' about the values but did not 'do' in accordance with what was expected. When feedback from individuals involved in the organization is perceived to support, and actual behaviour is congruent with, the values, only then can the organization be really certain that the values are shared. It is not enough simply to understand what the values should be, the architects of the culture must understand what the values are, and how they can be supported by specific actions and behaviours which are displayed by all members of the organization.

Linking values to the mission

Each individual's contribution to shaping the organization's culture will need to understand the values which support the mission. Individuals will also need to make the decision to 'buy in' to the values and thus internalize what they mean by being aware of the appropriate behaviours.

We need to recognize that it may take time for people to develop the skills of behaving naturally in a way which is congruent with the stated organizational values. To expect people to change quickly may be unreasonable. We need to take account of the pressure of the existing culture by recognizing that there may be many restraining factors lurking in the shadows only too ready to devalue change to a new culture.

For example, an organization we know seeks to develop its personnel by providing up-to-date training courses. The courses are normally well developed and executed by professional trainers. Yet feedback indicates that minimal benefits are derived by either the participants or the organization. A possible reason emerged when it was discovered that individuals perceived each course as top management's 'flavour of the month'. They also believed that they did not really need to absorb the new knowledge and skills as they would soon be replaced by the ideas from the next course. In addition they had experienced scepticism from middle management who, by their behaviour, discouraged them from implementing many of the skills covered by the courses.

Most developments to culture will need the dedicated effort and commitment of those who will shape the appropriate culture. We now know that it is not enough to understand at an intellectual level what is required; we need to 'buy into' the values and learn to live by them in the organization. Thus fulfilling both parts of the syndrome is vital to creating and reinforcing a desired culture.

SHARED VALUES

In organizational terms a value describes a desired mode of behaviour or practice which can be achieved when people understand, accept and use it to guide their thinking and actions. For example, if an organization decides that quality is of paramount value, it will need to be understood by individuals in terms they can relate to in their jobs. People need to understand what they have to do to achieve and maintain the desired performance standards which are perceived to be realistic and achievable.

As the organization achieves the desired quality standards

through the contribution made by its people, actions and behaviours which are consistent with the desired outputs are rewarded and reinforced. By being consistent in its actions, the organization will act in a manner which illustrates congruence thus encouraging its people to internalize the values which maintain quality standards.

We find the process of defining and establishing values a crucial part of an organization's strategy. Given that the mission will remain in place for a considerable period of time, the values may need to change. Time spent on identifying and defining the appropriate values provides ideal opportunities for all staff to be involved in shaping the organization's future. Individuals can generally relate to the concept of organizational values. However, some have difficulty in understanding how values affect the way they perform their jobs.

Culture and values

Organization culture comprises shared values which are established and reinforced by a range of components developed through the activities and behaviours of its leaders. Many of the components are woven into the informal fabric of the organization through unconscious as well as conscious actions. When developing a map of an organization's culture we look for actions and behaviours which are shown in Figure 8.1.

rituals	*language*	*humour*
norms	*class*	*dress*
myths	*structure*	*customs*

Figure 8.1 Organizational culture and values

In some organizations certain components can play a powerful role in shaping culture. We discovered in several organizations that humour was predominantly of a put-down nature and this resulted in individuals frequently being disabled. Yet within these organizations most of the managers felt the humour was acceptable as it fitted what they perceived to be the 'national' type of humour. Once they were aware of the demotivating effect it had on a significant number of individuals, managers modified their behaviour to eliminate the put-downs whilst retaining the more positive aspects of humour. This is only one of many examples of how 'normal' behaviour adversely impacts on organizational effectiveness.

Unwrapping an organization's culture can provide a valuable map of the values which exist. To be aware of the values can enable an organization to understand the action required to effect change. Being able to know what intervention strategy to use and to pinpoint the place and time can make the difference between effective and less effective change. Giving individuals the opportunity to explore what values exist in their organization can enable them to achieve a sound understanding of what the organization is in existence to achieve. Instead of it being some remote boss or group of bosses, they learn that its about them and is them. What they do in the performance of their jobs, in contact with others inside the organization, with customers and suppliers and during their non-work time is a reflection of the values. Through this level of awareness and understanding comes an internalized belief system which equips individuals to be responsible members of the organization by choice.

Living the values

It is generally understood that we cannot change our behaviour until we see and understand the benefits to be derived. The same is true when attempting to change an organization's culture. Unless it can create an environment based on a set of shared values expressed in terms which each individual can understand, relate to and perceive benefits, change is unlikely to take place. It is therefore vital, when involved in cultural change, to ensure that the development of values is a process which involves as many of the people in the organization as possible.

Involvement enables them to think through how each value relates to their own value system. It provides a real opportunity for differences to be discussed and a base of understanding to be achieved which enables them to accept ways they can express the values in their everyday lives. Acceptance is crucial as it provides individuals with the motivation to behave in a way which is congruent with the new culture being shaped. Once the appropriate behaviours are identified and individuals start using them, the process of shaping the new culture is under way.

Owning the values

A significant change in management practice over the past three years has centred on a process which enables individuals to feel that they can make a significant contribution to decision making which affects their individual as well as corporate lives. This encourages individuals to own the solution as theirs by accepting the outcome of the discussions as being mutually beneficial. A similar process needs to be applied when arriving at a culture of shared values. Sharing can be interpreted as owning the values in such a way that they are an internalized part of us. Therefore as we make our contribution within the organization we react in a way which is consistent with the developing culture, thus enhancing its real growth.

One of the significant steps associated with creating shared values is expressing the behaviours required in understandable terms. This means establishing standards/benchmarks by which individuals can relate their individual performance and thus identify how effectively they are living the values.

Setting relevant norms/standards

To illustrate what is required we consider several values which exist in an enabling organization. Each is dealt with briefly to provide insights into what should be expressed to help individuals understand what the values mean in behavioural terms. The values selected are key to the operation of an enabling environment:

- respect for others
- openness
- trust
- collaboration
- innovation.

One of the interesting and challenging aspects of shaping culture through the development of shared values is the language used. It often comes as a surprise to individuals to find that there are many different and divergent interpretations to quite simple words. Armed with this awareness enablers work to create a process which allows individuals to identify the values and express them in a language they understand. A real benefit of this process comes through the understanding achieved from the discussion of each value, rather than in the words used to describe them. The following examples illustrate the output from such discussions:

Respect for others

Describes the way we pay attention to what another person says and does. If we respect a person, we listen to what the person has to say and take account of the ideas expressed. We also respond in a positive manner irrespective of whether we accept or reject the information or advice. We aim to leave the person feeling that their contribution, whether requested or not, has been heard and understood.

Openness

Applies in a wide range of situations within our organization. It describes our individual willingness to disclose information and feeling based on respect and trust that it will be used in an appropriate and positive manner. Openness allows management to disclose much more information than normal as a strong bond of trust exists which, in turn, enables us to contribute more effectively to organizational goals.

Trust

Allows us to be open and take risks in disclosing information and sharing ideas with others in the organization. Trust is built on a foundation of individuals being accepted for what they are; being reliable in what they say and do; being consistent in ensuring that what they think, say and do agrees, as perceived by others.

Collaboration

Means active cooperation in that we seek ways to enhance the achievement of other individuals and units within our organization. The key to collaboration is through active involvement in the organization and a willingness to share and exchange ideas which will add value to all that each individual does.

Innovation

We understand innovation to mean the application of our efforts to find better and more effective ways to do our work which add value to the organization's outputs. Each of us can find ways to improve what we do and will share these with others to help them achieve better performance – just as they will do to assist us. It also means embracing new technology and finding ways for it to make an effective contribution to the organization.

Organizations have found that using a workshop approach to the development of culture and values has provided an excellent vehicle for achieving a high level of understanding. As understanding comes through discussion of what each value means and its relationship to individual behaviour, a significant number of individuals 'buy' them. This, in turn, provides the motivation and commitment to work to shape the desired culture.

The dynamic nature of an organization dictates that values need to be reviewed on a continuous basis to ensure they enable the organization to continue to be effective in different environments. Also, change comes in many different ways and the culture may require to be reinforced by modifying some of the values to take account of the changing circumstances. For example, change can create situations which are full of ambiguity and uncertainty in which some individuals find it difficult to cope. To combat this potentially negative effect, an organization can strive to create within its culture attitudes which view uncertainty and ambiguity in a positive manner.

Given that individuals in an organization have accepted and internalized the values which make up a positive, dynamic culture, they will be able to accommodate rapid change. Whatever the environment is in terms of change, the organization will be able to create the values which maintain its positive and dynamic response to keep it ahead in its field and maintain its overall effectiveness.

Historical culture

Although leaders tend to influence culture on a continuous basis, it is useful to note that in organizations much of the culture can be based on the past and may be out of touch with the needs of today and the future. The power of historical culture can often be seen by the way individuals fight to retain customs and practices which, although effective in their day, are no longer relevant. The attitudes expressed are genuine and firmly held and are often reinforced by the behaviour of certain leaders within the organization.

To attempt to change the attitudes and subsequent behaviour, it is imperative that the organization identify those values which need to be modified to enable change to take place. Once this has been done, strategies can be developed which enable people to modify their attitudes and behaviour in a positive way without feeling threatened and exposed.

However, if the values are not in tune with the mission or vice versa, the result may be dysfuntional behaviour and failure to achieve results.

Consequently enabling leadership's role within the organization is to work towards an environment which encourages individuals to be aware of the variances and to equip themselves with the ability to reshape the culture.

Changing values

As many organizations face the need to make changes, and often on a frequent basis, they will be anxious to identify what aspects of culture need to be modified to facilitate positive change. If individuals within the organization have bought into values of trust, openness, respect for others, accountability and consistency, the probability is high that they will also accept the value of flexibility, and therefore be open to change. To effect change an organization needs to work towards developing a culture which encourages its people to feel OK about change, to anticipate it in a positive manner and to be willing to work to achieve the change.

Returning to the case of the organization which used training to develop its people, individuals within the organization perceived training as an injection by senior management of a new toy every three months unrelated to their real world of work. Management appeared to fail to recognize that change in attitudes comes through a process which encourages individuals to identify their real development needs against a defined contribution. Once development needs have been identified, individuals are also provided with the opportunity to seek ways to fill the gaps.

Replacing senior management's imposed training with a participative process allows those involved to see the benefits from being better trained. This places a higher value on learning, resulting in change taking place as individuals are part of what emerges from the process, and they will also have a high degree of ownership of what happens.

Developing a culture which enhances the values needed to cope effectively with change requires careful thought and planning. Those leading change will need to ensure that their thinking, speaking and behaviour is continually congruent with the message they communicate about change. In most instances consistent behaviour by aware leaders provides the stimulus for people to accept change as a positive event. Once they act in a way which facilitates change, the organization is ready to reward and reinforce these positive behaviours. This process is aimed at moving the equilibrium from the past to the desired future state and then freezing it at the stage which represents the desired culture.

DEVELOPING INDIVIDUALS AND TEAMS

The thrust of this chapter has been in describing the type of environment which best represents an enabling organization. The picture which has emerged will be different for each reader based on their own individual mind set and openness to information which may differ from their views. To us, enabling organizations will have a driving desire to create an environment within which people are encouraged to grow and develop. The environment will enable people to determine whether they wish to advance or not, irrespective of proven ability, as the organization respects the individual.

As an overview of what we see to be an enabling organization we briefly describe several of its significant components:

- encourages individual growth
- openness and trust
- belief in people and their capability
- provides team-building opportunities
- multidisciplinary development
- focus on outputs and accountability.

Encouraging individual growth

Enabling leadership is very much centred on creating an environment and culture which encourages individuals within the organization to grow. One of the major components of the enabling leader's philosophy is that part concerned with empowering others. It recognizes that if the environment is constructive and people identify that they have the freedom to succeed (and fail) as a means of learning to grow, they will in fact accept the responsibility for their own individual growth.

The climate for individual growth will be constructed in such a way that each part will be congruent in achieving the desired goals. It means that all individuals will be willing to take risks and invest in their own individual development in a responsible and effective manner. It provides an opportunity for the enabling leader to encourage individuals to continue to improve their effectiveness within the broader framework of the organization's goals.

Individual development will be perceived in two ways. Namely, that of developing individual competence to perform as an individual as well as being able to work with others in a team. Teamwork will also be a recognized component of the environment as it is understood to be an effective way of enhancing individual growth. Enabling leadership will be concerned with obtaining the most effective benefits from a teamwork structure which recognizes individual and collective contributions.

Openness and trust

Individuals generally welcome the opportunity to operate within an open and trusting environment. They appreciate feedback which is designed to clarify and provide ideas for improvement. Difficult issues are confronted in a positive manner with honest feedback being given without disabling the individual concerned.

An open and trusting environment also requires individuals to be responsible. Disclosure and feedback will become more effective as the level of trust rises. Individuals will more readily accept critical feedback when they believe that it is given from a genuine desire to share perceptions. This sharing is accepted as a process designed to resolve differences and reach agreement on ways to improve personal and organizational effectiveness.

Belief in people and their capability

A major component of the climate is a belief in people. This belief encourages individuals to see themselves as responsible and capable. The enabling leader works at providing a framework of understanding which enables individuals to see how their current contribution fits organizational needs.

As the climate recognizes capability it adds to the other components which encourage individuals to put the necessary effort into achieving agreed outputs. It works on producing a clear understanding of the degree of effort each individual is required to make and how this links to the individual's capability. The enabling leader is very much concerned with encouraging each individual to be competent in terms of the application of skills and knowledge to meet the desired results. Competence is based on a belief that individuals will wish to act in a responsible manner because they have a clear understanding of how and where their contribution can be made.

Provides team-building opportunities

Within an enabling organization there will be many opportunities for real team development. This will be very relevant as organizations will be structured on a flexible basis to meet the challenge of change. Instead of being located in fixed departments for long periods of their career, individuals will find themselves being a part of many different teams, brought together for varying periods of time to meet specific objectives. These teams may be called project groups, task forces, problem-solving groups, brainstorming teams, etc.

An enabling leader will view each of these groups as an ideal opportunity for team-building and will recognize the most appropriate process to use, to enable the individuals to learn and grow from the experience. Being able to contribute in a team will be perceived as one of the key skills in the future and the enabling leader will create opportunities for learning, exchanging and sharing these skills.

Multidisciplinary development

One of the exciting opportunities of the future is provided in the exchanging process between individuals from different disciplines. Many organizations are now recognizing the value of the individual who has sound training as a generalist, which includes training in skills of adapting to meet specialist needs. This will provide teams of individuals with the capability of quickly learning new areas of knowledge and expertise to meet perceived or actual needs brought about by change.

Part of the learning and development process within the teams will be in their willingness to share and exchange knowledge and experience. This will be in contrast to the barriers erected in the past by individuals who feared change and sharing. As many of these groups will be of relatively short duration, with individuals being members of different groups, and an environment which encourages openness and trust, there will be a willingness to take calculated risks of a personal and business nature.

The recognition that risk is involved is accepted as an ongoing part of business and life. Individuals accept the part risk plays and understand that it requires to be handled in a responsible manner. By being aware of what they are attempting to accomplish, individuals have a high level of understanding of what they are accountable for. This sharpness of mission provides a sound framework for taking risk with an awareness of the potential consequences for others.

Focus on outputs and accountability

Within the positive environment described above individuals will be willing to take risks and modify their contributions accordingly. Modifications will be achieved in a positive manner because the risks will be established in terms of specific outputs. Therefore individuals will understand what they will be required to do to add value to the organization's goals.

They will be a part of shaping the outputs through a shared performance review process and therefore will be able to understand, in clear terms, the process involved in changing themselves and the organization to meet current and future needs.

The concentration on outputs is driven by an achievement orientation based on a belief in the ability of individuals to want to make significant contributions to an organization. An enabling organization provides by its mission and through its culture the sort of environment which encourages individual growth and development resulting in all individuals adding value in all that they do within the organization.

The next chapter presents a framework which enables individuals to understand their contribution to an organization and how best it can be delivered.

CONCEPTS EXPLORED IN CHAPTER 9

ENABLING CONTRIBUTION
INDIVIDUAL CONTRIBUTION
   Effort – Output – Reward
STRATEGY
   Values Driven
AIMS AND OBJECTIVES
   Directional Signposts
   Defining Objectives
   Contribution Profile
   Training in Contribution Profile (CP) System
ACHIEVEMENT FEEDBACK
   Achievement Review Process
   Achievement Agreement
   Sharing the Process
   Self-review
REWARD FOR CONTRIBUTION

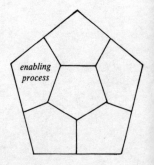

enabling process

9 Enabling process (2) – enabling contribution

ENABLING CONTRIBUTION

In Chapter 8 we described the characteristics of environments which provide involvement for individuals and generate the enthusiasm for them to make real contributions to their organization. The environment allows individuals to feel good about applying their skills, knowledge and experience to accomplish activities/tasks. It encourages them to be innovative and develop their abilities to improve achievement. Thus the outputs from all will be designed to add value to whatever they do to make the organization effective.

Contribution, which means 'to add to a common goal', is increasingly accepted as a term which accurately describes what individuals should 'make' to their organizations. It is a term which reflects the giving of one's skill, knowledge and experience in return for some benefit. The benefits may include money, status, security, glamour, satisfaction and fulfilment. Irrespective of the size and shape of the benefit, an individual can make a contribution in many different ways to meet his/her own personal needs and motivation. The aim of an organization is to enhance individual contributions by reaching agreement with each individual on what he/she can do to add to the common goal.

An organization needs to provide a framework to enable individuals to understand the role and contribution they can make. Such a framework is illustrated in Figure 9.1.

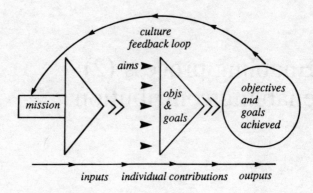

Figure 9.1   Framework for contribution

An organization has a responsibility to provide clear direction by explaining what it aims to achieve. It also has a responsibility in assisting individuals understand what contribution they are expected to make. To be certain that a particular result will be achieved requires careful planning and direction. People need to know what is expected of them, when and to what standard. To achieve a satisfactory basis of understanding an organization can devise participative processes to cover the following key components:

- individual contribution
- strategy
- aims and objectives
- performance feedback
- rewards for contribution.

An enabling organization has the ability to involve its people in shaping and reinforcing its culture. Coupled to this, enabling leaders can develop processes to encourage individuals to understand what their contribution is and how best it can be made.

INDIVIDUAL CONTRIBUTION

Enabling leaders recognize the value of tapping into the knowledge, experience and awareness individuals have about their jobs. By inviting them to contribute ideas, value can be added to the organization's effectiveness. This recognition provides a vehicle for encouraging individuals to feel free to share their ideas, perceptions and experiences in an open and positive way designed to improve performance.

To achieve this an enabling organization provides opportunities for individuals to be involved in putting shape and purpose to the contribution they make. This requires them to be responsible for their actions and encourages them to use their skills and knowledge to improve individual and organizational effectiveness.

Enabling leaders encourage individuals to think about how they can improve their achievement and thus enhance their contribution to the organization. Enablers understand that, when individuals believe their views are welcomed and respected, they will act in a responsible manner and will accept personal accountability for the contribution they make. As this contribution is made within an environment of individual and team work, it raises possibilities for individuals to share ideas designed to improve individual and team effectiveness.

Effort – output – reward

A primary aim of enabling leadership is to encourage individuals, as an individual or within teams, to accept responsibility for their contribution to the organization. In return their contribution is recognized by the team and organization in relation to its value to the total output achieved. An enabling organization ensures that effort, as expressed by the contribution made (which adds value) to the organization's outputs, will be directly linked to the reward the individual receives.

Part of the shift in management practice now taking place is in providing individuals with a clear understanding of what is expected from them as their contribution. This is achieved in different ways, from being set out in job descriptions developed by management to a completely integrated process which involves each manager and team members. We have experience of a wide range of processes and will describe later in the chapter a process entitled 'Contribution Profile' which is integrative and participative.

To assist individuals understand what they are expected to contribute involves constructing an environment which recognizes that individuals have a contribution to make; often in their own unique ways. Also, it will see the contribution as being valuable irrespective of the position an individual holds. To assist the process the following criteria should be considered:

- The contribution should be explained in a context of the part it plays in meeting the organization's mission, aims and objectives. The picture should, therefore, be a 'wide screen' one to enable the individual to obtain a sense how he/she 'fits' in the process of things.
- The individual should be aware of the skill, knowledge, experience and attitudes required to make the contribution effectively.
- Who the individual will have as 'clients' within the organization should be clear and their specific requirement expressed in observable/measurable terms.
- Those who provide information, materials and services to the individual should also be identified and the how/what of their contribution should be understood in observable/measurable terms.
- The dynamic nature of the organization needs to be explained to enable the individual to understand the degree of flexibility required in their contribution.
- An agreement of what the individual is expected to contribute would be produced encompassing all the key inputs required to produce specified outputs. This would also describe the behavioural characteristics of the job and what is expected from the individual. These would all be congruent with the organization's mission, aims and objectives.
- A process would be established to provide feedback on actual achievement, as the contribution is being made. The process would be continuous and woven into day-to-day management, and agreed by the parties concerned.

The whole process will require a significant investment of time and effort to achieve the best results. When done with conviction and a real desire to achieve true understanding of what is expected from an individual, the actual outputs can be outstanding. It also provides a fine opportunity for individuals to learn about and influence culture by inputting insights from their perceptions of what has been learned during the process.

Experience shows that much less time is required, following the initial investment, in assisting individuals understand how they can make their contribution. Because individuals have been involved in an unwrapping process their understanding of what the organization is and how it achieves is very high. Organizations recognize the level of awareness and continue to provide opportunities for the individual to be kept informed and involved in shaping their future.

STRATEGY

All organizations need a focus on what they are attempting to achieve through their very existence. They tend to produce some form of plan which indicates the outputs expected from the investment of a variety of resources. Plans often contain a number of statements which describe how the resources are to be deployed and what return is expected from the effort expended. The degree of detail will vary depending on what management needs to give it a clear picture of the future.

Plans are developed from a clear sense of what exists and what may exist in the future. Being able to paint scenarios of the future based on determined variables can provide insights into new strategic directions the organization should take. Strategic planning is central to an enabling organization's thrust into the future. Its desire to build awareness of the possibilities in terms of new markets, products and services leads it to undertake a wide range of activities to secure insights into what the future may hold.

Analysis of the information gleaned from environmental scanning can provide insights into potentially beneficial trends in the economic, social, environmental, political and behavioural spheres of influence. An outcome from strategic thinking is the creation of a shared vision of the future. When achieved through a consultative process involving senior managers it provides an ideal launching pad for new initiatives to keep the organization ahead. Although surprising changes in direction may result from the process, leaders and managers are aware and ready to implement what is required from their understanding and commitment to the new direction(s).

Interest in the future gives enabling leaders a forward-looking orientation. They are interested in attempting to understand what the future may hold and how their organization can position itself to gain the best possible advantage. Therefore, developing strategies is one of the important ways of shaping the future. One type of process enabling leaders use was described in Chapter 2. They develop their own strategic models to enable them to make sense of internal and external environmental scanning. This enables them to be proactive in their approach and thus keep their organization in the forefront of its field of endeavour.

As the pace of change accelerates enabling leaders need to maintain their awareness of what is happening in the 'marketplace'. Being successful requires a keen sense of what gives the organization its competitive advantage. The key components of competitive advantage will be understood and relate to what makes the organization successful. Congruence will exist between the mission, shared values, strategic direction and objectives the organization is following.

Values driven

Any change in direction would necessitate a thorough review of the mission statement to ensure the two were still congruent. If not, the mission statement would be amended to take account of the changing circumstances using a participative process to ensure organizational members understood the reasons for change and were able to relate to them. In this way enabling leaders would secure a high level of 'buy-in' to the new mission with resulting commitment.

In our view the presence of an accepted mission provides an organization with a heart and soul to which its members can relate. We refer to the mission for XYZ organization described in Chapter 8 to enable us to examine this further:

> XYZ is committed to providing quality products and services which meet customers' needs and provides them with value for money. We will work in an open, collaborative and innovative manner to enable us to produce and deliver our products and services in an effective and courteous way.

We then produced a list of values drawn from the mission statement. It is these values which provide clear signposts to organizational members on how the organization plans to achieve its objectives. They flag the key issues of quality, customer need, value for money, delivered on time and in a courteous manner, innovation and team working through collaboration. The values need to be clearly stated to enable everyone to relate their personal values to what the organization espouses as its values, thus ensuring that all members are aware of what is expected in their contribution to fulfil the key components.

The value statements form a sound foundation on which the organization can build and develop its people resource. The possession of a clear and well-understood organizational philosophy provides strength in moving on to the next important stage. We say that all organizations need to have strategic directions which point to where they are going and what they expect to achieve from the utilization of their resources.

Strategic directions will be expressed by an organization in a manner which effectively communicates what it aims to achieve in the future. Using a little poetic licence, we have extracted from the above mission statement examples of what we describe as organizational aims.

AIMS AND OBJECTIVES

Before listing the aims it may be useful to describe what we perceive an aim should express. An aim should state clearly what the organization plans to achieve over a given period of time, say two to three years. We found some confusion in organizations over the interpretation and use of aims and objectives. In many instances the two were used to describe the same thing. From experience we find that an objective represents an activity which can be achieved in a relatively short period of say up to one year. Whereas, as stated above, an aim can exist for many years. The differences should become clearer as we explore them in more depth.

With a little creative interpretation, the following aims were identified:

- to provide opportunities for people to grow and develop, and be rewarded in relation to the contribution they make to the organization
- to provide an environment which encourages people to make an effective contribution which enables synergy to be achieved
- to be an innovative organization committed to producing quality products and distributing them to customers in effective ways
- to be No. 1 in our market through the quality, reliability and value for money of our products
- to generate a level of profit which enables the organization to grow and develop in an effective manner which provides an adequate ROI for both shareholders and employees.

The way we have listed and expressed the aims represents a major difference in organizational thinking. In most cases organizations start their aims with a declaration that growth and profit is their prime purpose for being in business. We question this thinking as in our view organizations are in business to produce and sell products and/or services to meet customers' needs. The skills and techniques used by its people, coupled with the strategy it adopts to differentiate its outputs from others, will determine to a major extent its degree of growth and subsequent level of profits.

Our interpretation shifts the focus onto the people who make up the organization and on the skills, knowledge and experience they contribute. In recent times, we observe that organizations are beginning to place increasing emphasis on the development of people as a means of developing the organization. This is an important concept which if continued would significantly influence the value of contribution made.

Directional signposts

The aims should provide a set of clear signposts which point to the direction the organization is planning to take and to which its members can relate. Aims also provide direction to management as they shape strategy, policies and procedures which allow the organization to operate. They emphasize the philosophy which promotes the value of each individual, whether working as an individual or in teams, as they add value to everything the organization does.

Enablers work within organizations to encourage the development of a mission statement which encapsulates the enabling philosophy. In turn, the enabling philosophy captures the spirit of equality and respect for the individual. This accounts for the fact that the aim of successful organizations is to develop processes which enable them to harness, in a positive way, the creative potential of their people resource.

When individuals are involved in the development of the aims, and their translation into individual objectives/goals, they are more likely to be committed to their achievement. This process provides them with the opportunity to own and accept responsibility for the contribution they make. It creates a climate which recognizes the value of people being self-managed and self-directed with high awareness of others' needs. The main thrust, therefore, in developing aims, and of involving people in the process, is to provide direction and thus enhance the establishment of appropriate objectives to which each individual can relate.

Defining objectives

The second aim of our enabling organization is to create an environment which encourages people to make an effective contribution. To have this aim fulfilled the organization would develop a framework with the following three sub-aims:

- develop objectives to state clearly what the organization expects to achieve by the end of a given period, e.g. the one-year business plan

- develop a process which enables the objectives to be translated by/for every individual within the organization
- provide a process which recognizes the value of each individual's contribution and rewards accordingly.

An objective should be a statement which describes the output(s) expected from an activity or individual in measurable/observable terms. To illustrate the output orientation and descriptive nature of an objective we have drawn up the following example from an administrative section:

- 'To hold an information exchange session of approximately 30 minutes with senior staff (attendee list to be agreed with dept. heads) from all administrative departments at 9.00 on the first Tuesday of each month between February and May, and August to December, with the purpose of keeping them informed on policy and operational changes.'

An objective should leave no doubts about what is to be achieved and when. The 'how' is left to the team or individual to determine once the objectives have been agreed.

We therefore need to be aware that individuals and teams in an organization will develop their objectives using different perspectives and timeframes. The chief executive and executive team will have a fairly long-term focus and will tend to establish objectives which reflect a macro-view of what they wish to achieve. For example, they may set an objective to raise their turnover to £130 million in the next financial year. For this objective to be achieved, management will need to reach agreement on the objectives which spell out in specific detail the required contribution of each individual involved in the organization. Whilst senior managers tend to take a long-term view, we perceive that the closer individuals are to the action the more they tend to develop a short-term focus as their concerns are usually about next month, week or day.

The state of health of the organization will also influence the degree to which the focus is long term. Managers who are pressurized to meet perceived short-term goals become very adept at putting out bushfires. If and when the situation changes and they have no fires to fight some experience real difficulty in making the adjustment to a planning mode of operation. The following comments were recently stated by two expert firefighters, 'I am so busy I don't have time to set objectives', and, 'Things are so chaotic around here! It would be a waste of valuable time to do any real planning.' These comments indicate attitudes which devalue the planning process, perpetuate ineffectiveness, and have an unfortunate habit of becoming part of the organization's informal culture.

Working to achieve clarity of mission, aims and objectives by involving people in the shaping of their objectives is an important role for the enabling leader. The process is successfully completed when individuals can relate their objectives and goals to the major objectives set by the organization. This is recognized as a sound process by which an organization can encourage individuals to be committed to fulfilling their objectives through understanding and acceptance of how they contribute to the corporate objectives. When accomplished effectively the outcome is a simple and understandable set of goals which individuals can 'buy' and deliver.

The vital ingredient in setting objectives is to ensure that everyone involved in achieving the objectives is able to relate to, and accept responsibility for, the outcome. This means that each manager negotiates and agrees objectives with his/her leader before using a similar process with his/her team. When agreeing objectives, we learned from many managers that they used a framework which enabled both parties to understand the key steps in the process. The steps are:

- clarify what has to be done in specific observable/measurable terms
- assess the 'fit' of an individual's capability to make an effective contribution
- reach agreement on outputs and achievement standards
- agree feedback process to ensure both parties are aware of actual achievement and to take account of influencing factors
- establish benefits expected from contribution made to agreed achievement standards.

Managers found the framework assisted them in obtaining clarity about what each individual could contribute. They also understood what they were required to do to support the efforts of

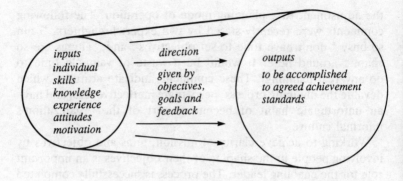

Figure 9.2   Contribution process model

their team. They found it was necessary to use a language which everybody understood. To assist understanding and provide a sharp focus it may be appropriate to use different terms for objectives. This allows individuals to express objectives in a language which relates to the actual situation they experience in performing their jobs.

To differentiate between the macro- and micro-objectives we could call objectives those activities which will take over six months to accomplish, ones with a shorter duration of say 3 – 6 months could be termed targets. Whilst activities which can be accomplished within three months could be called goals. The main advantage of using agreed terminology is to help individuals relate what is agreed in their objectives to the timeframes required to achieve their particular part of the required outputs.

It is well worth investing time to obtain a clarity in setting and agreeing objectives. The time will be amply rewarded by the commitment to see the goals achieved because the individual 'owns' them.

We have developed a participative process to meet the need and secure commitment to a common direction and outcome.

Contribution profile

The process starts with management understanding that the Contribution Profile (CP) System has the following requirements

- commitment to a participative processs resulting in goals being agreed and accepted by all individuals
- willingness to invest the time and resources necessary to undertake the process in an effective manner
- existence of, or desire for, a culture of collaboration, achievement, openness and trust.

The process can commence once the organization accepts and is committed to the investment described above. It will normally commence with the top management group to ensure they understand the process and have effectively established their goals in relation to the corporate objectives.

The Contribution Profile System comprises the following stages.

Stage 1

Completion of profile by the individual prior to session with manager. Manager will have already completed his/her own profile which has been accepted by his/her team leader.

Stage 2

Meeting with manager to discuss CP and reach agreement on the outputs for an agreed period. The process may require more than one session to ensure a satisfactory CP emerges.

Stage 3

The CP is circulated to the jobholder's 'clients' for their perusal and comment. Where differences are identified they would be discussed by the individuals to reach a satisfactory solution. Contact would be made by the jobholder with 'suppliers' who did not emerge from this stage of the process.

Stage 4

Comments from 'clients and suppliers' would be considered by the manager and jobholder to reach agreement on the modifications required to meet their needs. Discussions between departments may be required to resolve areas of difference in expectations.

Once completed the individual's CP would be agreed and become operational for the agreed period.

Stage 5

Review of contribution on an agreed basis to provide feedback on achievement and take account of factors, beyond the individual's control, which may affect achievement of the goals.

Stage 6

Develop reward systems to ensure contributions, which meet or exceed agreed goals, are adequately recompensed. The system should enable the organization to reward commensurate with the effort contributed. We recommend that a reward package be agreed at this stage to enable individuals to know what will be given in return for their contribution.

The system requires a number of working papers to enable individuals to establish their profiles and build its relevance to others within the organization. Initial focus is on developing a clear understanding of what each individual is required to contribute to achieve corporate goals. This is done by encouraging each individual to focus on several key factors in his/her job. Individuals are invited to:

● describe in one or two sentences the purpose of their job in terms of what it does to add value to the organization
● describe the main goals they have which account for at least 80 per cent of their job
● consider each main goal and list any sub-goals which need to be accomplished to fulfil achievement of the main goal
● name who their 'clients' are within the organization, i.e. those people to whom their job provides a service
● take each sub-goal and describe what their named 'clients' would perceive to be the 'success criteria' of the service provided
● name the 'suppliers' of service to them and describe the success criteria used to determine that their service is effective.

A simple point and weighting system is used to clarify which of the main goals and sub-goals are significant enough to be included in the profile. The development of the profile will involve individuals, team leaders, clients and suppliers. It is a highly participative process which produces a very high level of understanding of what each individual contributes to the organization.

Training in the Contribution Profile (CP) System

We encourage organizations to develop their own CPs as this results in greater ownership of the process. They will design working-sheets and establish the steps in the process. We recommend that the process should start with top management and that training should be provided. In our experience the investment in effective training has produced significant benefits in developing a collaborative culture with results orientation.

Taking time out from the workplace has been accepted as an effective means of achieving a real understanding of the process and it outputs. In an off-site workshop setting the top management group is involved in individual and small group work designed to take them through each stage of the CPS. When participants have finished their individual profile, they are involved in a project of examining what the chief executive has produced and how it relates to the corporate goals. Modifications are made to take account of variances due to missing goals or ones which should be the responsibility of someone else.

The next stage involves a group review of the other profiles to ensure linkage between the chief executive's CP and each individual's CP on the executive team. As this process continues, it tends to highlight areas of uncertainty regarding what each individual should do. Grey areas can be identified and specific goals allocated to the individual primarily responsible for the outcome. Where two or more have a similar goal the process allows a clearer understanding of what should be done, by whom and when. Modifications to a profile are only made with the full agreement of the individual concerned.

Once satisfied with their profiles the senior management team then work with their own teams. A workshop approach is beneficial for all individuals required to produce a CP. Mixing staff from different departments and disciplines provides ideal opportunities for cross-fertilization. It also enables individuals to learn of the different perceptions which can exist between 'clients and suppliers' within their organization. Being able to discuss these differences in an open manner provides real opportunities for solutions to be found which enhance contributions and improve achievement.

Feedback from workshops indicate that the following issues arise and can be effectively dealt with:

- a tendency to confuse aims with objectives
- difficulty in writing objectives which are measurable/-observable, particularly for administrative and support functions
- discovery that too many goals are produced which have minimal impact on the outputs of a job and which deflect attention from the real key goals
- recognition of a strong tendency for managers to include their team members' goals in their own profiles
- discovery of significant differences between what some managers perceive they should contribute to a 'client', either within their team or in another area, when compared with identified needs
- difficulty of seeing goals as outputs and in envisioning what the end result will be like
- benefit of having a mission and values as a framework from which benchmarks can be established on the quality of inputs required to achieve goals.

Once the objectives and goals have been agreed, the next stage involves developing an agreed process to provide feedback on achievement. Any process needs to take account of the factors which may influence achievement of the objectives and which are outwith the individuals' direct control. The aim is to provide a climate of openness which enables individuals to keep in touch with what is happening as it happens. To ensure this we perceive that the process will be continuous and woven into each person's job.

Using a participative process, such as the CPS, within an appropriate culture, provides an organization with a framework to enable it to achieve clarity of purpose, commitment to contribution and convergence of effort to achieve its corporates goals. As individuals strive to accomplish their objectives, feedback provides the opportunity to identify those factors which could influence achievement and modify the objectives as required. Recognizing the potential complexity of an objective-setting process stimulates enabling leaders to encourage active participation coupled with genuine feedback on achievement.

ACHIEVEMENT FEEDBACK

An important part of the enabling process involves providing an opportunity for individuals to identify how effective their contribution is. Therefore, the main aims of an achievement review process should be:

- to create an environment where individuals understand and accept the relevance of their contribution
- to encourage individuals to want to continue to improve their own and the organization's achievement for the benefit of all
- to provide recognition and reward for individual contribution.

In an enabling organization feedback is based on a review of achievement against agreed and understood output criteria. Achievement is therefore not appraised in the traditional way by a manager judging what a subordinate has done. It is a shared exploration, of the contribution being made, by an individual and his/her team leader to understand how effective it is in meeting agreed goals.

Enabling leaders understand that individuals require feedback on what is being done and how well it meets the required performance standards. This provides an individual with information on what is happening and with the choice of what he/she should do in response. The importance of feedback is in its ability to assist individuals obtain a clear understanding on issues in which they are involved, or have a direct interest.

Achievement review processes should help people learn to receive feedback in a positive way, irrespective of its content. Individuals are encouraged to avoid being 'hooked' emotionally by feedback which is mainly positive or negative. It is so easy to

become high on good feedback or depressed and angry with negative comments. The skill is in hearing and understanding what is
being said and relating it to one's own views on the issue. Where
there is a lack of clarity, the individual needs to ask for specific
examples of actions or behaviours which illustrate what is being
said. The process will be successful when it enables individuals to
feel that they possess a clear understanding on all issues which
relate to their contribution.

When the work environment is one which encourages openness
and trust, individuals will become more willing to take the risk of
disclosing and discussing perceived development needs which
affect their contribution. Enabling leadership aims to develop such
an environment within which individuals feel free and able to
express views in a constructive manner. The sharing and exchange
of ideas will therefore be done as a means of improving individuals
and team effectiveness. Individuals will be willing to express their
ideas with the aim of providing constructive comment to enhance
their achievement and that of others.

Reviewing achievement provides individuals with the opportunity to examine their perceptions against the perception of
others. Although they may feel that a satisfactory contribution
has been made, this view may not in fact be shared by others.
Feedback should therefore be provided in a constructive manner
designed to enable individuals test their reality against the reality
of others. And from the testing, to increase awareness of how
effective their contribution has been. Feedback can also provide
insights into the areas individuals need to improve to enhance
their contribution. In addition, it provides inputs on, and opportunities for, development to meet future challenges.

Achievement review process

An effective achievement review process provides individuals with
information which enables them to understand the effectiveness
of their contribution. It also provides clarity around what may be
the main constituents of the contribution. Through feedback and
discussion the shape and size of their contribution will be explored
in terms of the skills, knowledge and attitudes which they need
to apply to make it happen. As organizations are generally

involved in dynamic environments it becomes important for individuals to receive feedback which relates achievement to the ongoing situation. For an achievement review process to be effective it needs to be continuous. In many situtions individuals are expected to achieve results which are significantly influenced by factors outside their direct control. As achievement reviews are carried out against understood and acceptable measurable/-observable outputs, such external and internal influences will be identified and their effect on the individuals' contribution understood. An achievement review process conducted on an ongoing basis can identify, take account of and plan to obtain the best results possible from any of these unexpected influencing factors.

Achievement agreement

Continuous monitoring of achievement means that it needs to be structured to provide regular feedback opportunities. The enabling leader will aim to achieve a clear understanding with members of his/her team of the part their contribution makes to the results required.

The result of shared discussion and understanding could be termed an achievement agreement which each party understands and accepts as representing what is expected from them. The contribution profile is an example of how an agreement can be reached and how it provides a sound foundation on which to base an achievement review. The agreement also takes account of the environment within which the individual will make the contribution and any other issues which may have a potentially positive/negative influence on results.

An achievement agreement will include agreement on how feedback will be carried out to meet the needs of those involved. The performance review process is designed to enable all parties to contribute feedback. Its main aim is to provide a framework which enables individuals to make an effective contribution. An effective achievement review process allows each individual to get on with the job with the minimum of supervision and interference and a clear understanding of how the job interrelates with others.

Sharing the process

An enabling organization encourages individual and team responsibility in making a contribution. This involves considerable collaboration, sharing and exchanging designed to add value to all that is done. It is therefore natural in this environment for an achievement review process to be a shared activity.

Working together to understand what needs to be done in a job creates an ideal opportunity for sound relationships to grow. With mutual respect and a desire to achieve results all issues can be handled in an enabling manner. This provides a scope for individuals to raise issues about another person's activities and behaviours when they impinge on their own contribution. In a constructive environment these issues can be raised and resolved in a positive and non-threatening manner.

An enabling achievement review process encourages individuals to share perceptions on their contribution and its effectiveness. There are considerable benefits to be derived from tapping into the wealth of ideas held by team members. Individuals doing a particular job tend to be aware of how it could be improved. We also discovered that after only a short time working in a team they develop a high awareness on how the team's effort can be improved to raise its effectiveness.

Suspending judgements is an important part of the sharing process. It allows others to feel accepted and indicates in a powerful way that the manager is listening and is receptive to information. This opens many doors to discovery as new concepts can emerge when individual minds are free to express their thoughts. One organization we know encourages all individuals, irrespective of length of service and experience, to comment on any issue which they believe could improve achievement and add value. Several of its accountants suggested ways the marketing and sales departments could make their calls and sales support effort more effective. The ideas were well received and after further discussion several were implemented resulting in improved effectiveness.

Releasing individuals and organizations from the bondage of their historical past can provide many benefits. In most instances it is the informal culture which influences individuals to be closed and uncooperative. Recognizing its negative power, and instituting interventions designed to transform it into a more open and cooperative culture, is vital. It will not take long for individuals to relearn how to collaborate in an open environment which helps them improve individual and organizational effectiveness.

Creating an environment which encourages individuals to share in a genuine and open manner without becoming defensive is the enabler's aim. As trust builds and individuals understand the goal-setting and performance review process, they will have a better picture of how well they are achieving.

Self-review

As the achievement review process is a shared responsibility designed to achieve specific outputs it should encourage individuals to be able to conduct a self-review. This requires an individual to review objectively his/her achievements against the agreed objectives prior to a meeting to discuss the results.

Review meetings would be concerned with reaching understanding on what needs to be done in the future. The review may only take a few minutes when the perception of both parties is as one and they agree on what action, if any, is required.

Counselling mode

Where differences in perception exist, the enabling leader would conduct the review session using a counselling mode (described in Chapter 7). This mode is designed to explore the differences, from the individual's point of view, in an attempt to unwrap the issues which appear to cause the difference. A counselling process will assist differences to narrow as understanding of each individual's position increases.

The enabling leader senses what the best approach will be to reach agreement with an individual or group. Using developmental counselling can help create a climate which encourages individuals to think through the issues constructively. The outcome can be very rewarding as individuals learn to think for themselves and take responsibility for their actions.

Using a shared process in setting goals and being able to receive feedback gives individuals a clear picture of how well they are doing. Adjustments to performance can then be made and in the end the required results should be achieved. At this stage the individual should receive the appropriate recognition from his/her contribution.

REWARD FOR CONTRIBUTION

As essential component of enabling leadership is in creating a process of rewards appropriate to an individual's contribution/needs. Enabling organizations seek to develop reward processes which ensure that individuals receive recognition for their contribution. This will be based on a shared review and agreement of the value of the contribution to the organization's overall goals. Value may be expressed in different ways but will be recognized and accepted by the individual as fair and appropriate. This will involve the organization offering a range of benefits which enables individuals to select a package specifically to meet their needs.

We have observed many individuals giving significant contributions who were content to receive expressions of appreciation in return. In other instances contributions, if they could be called that, were little and given with poor grace - and the reward expected far outweighed its value to the organization. If we focus on the contribution a person agrees to make to an organization, and agree a value for its successful completion, the outcome should be satisfactory to both parties. In our view this process challenges the current concept of groups of people being paid the same rate for the job; in many instances, irrespective of the quality of the contribution.

As society changes from an industrial to an information one we shall witness many changes in the way we work. In fact, the oppotunity to work is becoming a privilege for many. Yet one of the paradoxes of today lies in the fact that there is so much to be done to improve the quality of life and provide development opportunities for anyone who wishes to make a contribution. We can provide 'work' for all those who want to 'work' by making a transition from the present antiquated processes which resist change, and replacing them with processes based on a contribution model. This will allow individuals to make a contribution in many different ways including voluntary contributions. The desired return would be agreed to match the quality and value of the contribution to the organization, with the contribution and reward being agreed through a full participative process.

An enabling organization seeks to make the transition from the past to the future and to provide effective processes which enable its members to feel good about its direction and effectiveness. Making the transition effective requires an environment which encourages individuals to want to find solutions to key issues, encourages creativity and actively reinforces behaviours which provide unique solutions and actions which move the organization forward in the agreed direction. The energy and commitment contributed by its members will see a transformation which encompasses the best practices required to keep the organization effective.

CONCEPTS EXPLORED IN CHAPTER 10

How to Enable Change
THE CHANGE PROCESS
  Influences On Our Attitudes
  Change Process Model
  Reactions to Change
THE NEED FOR POSITIVE ATTITUDES
  Investment in the Majority
  Positive Attitudes
CHANGE STARTS WITH THE INDIVIDUAL
  Making Decisions and Receiving Feedback
POINTS OF INTERVENTION
  Indicators
  Strategic Directions
  Seeking Opportunities
  Solution-seeking
  Points of Intervention
  Awareness of the Need to Intervene
  Purpose of Intervention
ENABLING CHANGE
  Helping Others Cope With Change

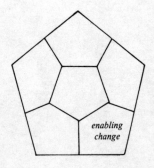

enabling change

10 Enabling change

We discussed in an earlier chapter the importance of self-awareness and the effect of change on the process. When thinking about change there is a tendency for individuals to feel negative about its effects. We appear to relate change to incidents and issues which can cause pain, for example, illness, redundancy, divorce. This feeling can colour our thinking and create an internal reaction which generates fear when we encounter any change.

Enablers start from a position of accepting that change is continuous and inevitable. By accepting this position, they focus on being aware of what change means and how it happens. The attitude they develop is one of anticipating the opportunities change offers and not being fearful of its effects.

Today the rate of change appears to be accelerating. The time taken for an idea to become a reality through improvement in technological development is becoming shorter as each year passes. The effects on industry, commerce and society in general mean that people have less time to adapt to change and feel bad about its effects. Enabling means accepting that there will be uncertainty and ambiguity surrounding the outcome of change but also accepting that in every change situation there will be opportunities for growth and development.

How to enable change

In this chapter we examine the concept and practice of enabling change by exploring the change process and its potential under the following components:

- the change process
- the need for positive attitudes
- change starts with the individual
- points of intervention
- enabling change.

THE CHANGE PROCESS

We shall explore the change process to understand what change is, its effects and how we can handle these in a positive manner.

We start by exploring the current situation to understand why its effects are interpreted in mainly negative forms. We shall touch on the following areas:

- influences on our attitudes
- change process model
- reactions to change.

Influences on our attitudes

Many of us develop a natural resistance to change because we perceive its effects on society and on us to be negative. We are continually influenced by events largely – both national and local – which appear to have disastrous effects. Although many of these events may not touch us directly, we often feel the effect because of the way information about them is communicated. There seems to be a strong belief held by the media that the population prefers hearing bad news to good news. Consequently we are bombarded (if we choose to be) with much that is wrong and negative about people and society. Television can be a powerful force as it:

- reflects and affects attitudes

- focuses on and reinforces behaviours
- legitimizes and perpetuates myths
- portrays and reinforces stereotypes.

Think about how television and other media portray the following events which cause or are the result of change:

- structural change
- organizational change
- technological change
- career upheavals
- societal pressures
- unemployment/underemployment
- international competition
- individual rights
- environmental issues
- political pressures.

Given the tendency to focus on the negative and the power to influence attitudes, it should not be hard to understand why many of us react defensively to any sort of change.

Change process model

When we explore change, it is with a view to understanding what it is, why it happens and what we need to do to cope with its effects. The following model describes in simple terms what takes place in the change process.

The change process commences when the individual identifies, perceives or is influenced by some trigger event. Trigger events can range from those which affect a person's physical, social, mental, spiritual or psychological states. These can range from being small and imperceptible to large and mind blowing. Examples of trigger events include:

- promotion
- redundancy
- lottery win
- death of a close relative/friend

- passing an exam
- injury which affects ability
- birth of a child
- middle-age crisis
- new job.

Some of these have a major impact on an individual whilst others may have little effect. However, change will start to take place only when the individual feels or perceives the need to change. The attitudes an individual forms in relation to the felt/perceived need for change will shape how well that person manages the change event.

Motivation to change will be expressed in one of two ways: positively or negatively. If approached with a positive attitude, the person will create a positive vision and identify what is needed to achieve a new and satisfactory situation. Subsequent action will be congruent and designed to achieve the vision with feedback helping to modify actions until the end result fits the vision. Once a person feels all right, the new attitudes and behaviours will become internalized, thus reinforcing a positive attitude to change and enabling the individual to face future trigger events with confidence (Figure 10.1).

On the other hand, if the attitudes adopted are negative, motivation to change will be replaced by a desire to resist change and retain the status quo. The individual's response could be to defend the position through using behaviours which are perceived as

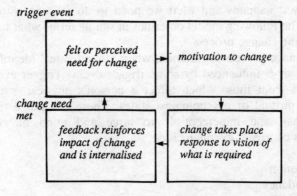

Figure 10.1   Positive change process

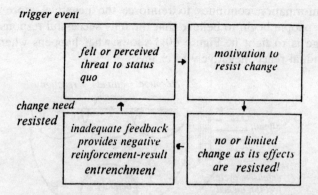

Figure 10.2   Negative change process

attacking or withdrawing. The outcomes are likely to be as negative as the attitudes held by the individual (Figure 10.2).

The remaining phases of the process are thus contaminated by the attitudes which reinforce themselves in a self-fulfilling manner. Individuals are therefore likely to be further mentally disabled, with fear of future trigger events being reinforced.

Reactions to change

Understanding the change process offers us the opportunity to determine how we might respond to achieve the best result when confronted with the need to change. In most instances we have the *choice* of responding either negatively or positively to the triggers for change. In a society which is fed on a diet of negative inputs about change, it is fairly predictable to expect unhelpful and unhealthy attitudes. This process provides powerful conditioning and produces the following attitudes:

- fear of the anticipated and unexpected
- uncertainty and discontinuity
- fear of losing control
- disaffiliation
- helplessness and hopelessness resulting in apathy
- antipathy and hostility
- 'head in the sand'.

As information continues to reinforce the negative, more and more people begin to believe that the only successful response to change is to fight it. Figure 10.3 shows what happens when an individual reacts negatively to change.

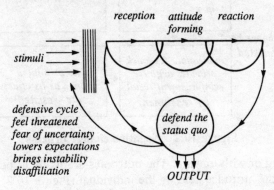

reception   attitude   reaction
forming

stimuli

defensive cycle
feel threatened
fear of uncertainty
lowers expectations
brings instability
disaffiliation

defend the status quo

OUTPUT

Figure 10.3   Defensive cycle

Once individuals enter a defensive cycle their ability to perceive the reality of the situation is increasingly reduced because of clogging of their perceptual filters. As they react against change defensive attitudes are reinforced by the following factors:

- previous experience (historical baggage)
- value and belief system
- habit and inertia
- pressure to conform
- no incentive to change
- poor self-image
- comfort in the past.

It may appear from the description of the results and corresponding negative reactions to change that the task of encouraging people to respond positively would be almost impossible. This is a challenge the enabling leader faces with confidence, enthusiasm, a sound belief and vision of a positive future. An enabling leader will understand why individuals respond negatively to change and will relate to them with empathy and understanding. Relationships will be based on an attempt to understand where each individual is and the factors which cause individuals to feel and act as they do towards change.

THE NEED FOR POSITIVE ATTITUDES

A powerful vision developed by enablers focuses on the benefits derived from investing energy and effort into developing the majority of individuals. They include those who may feel ambivalent about change to those who perceive its positive possibilities. Their vision comes from an awareness of the enormous effort contributed by society to contain and discipline the negative deviants, as described in Chapter 2. The outcome from this massive investment tends to adds further restrictions to the 'rights' of the majority resulting in increasing apathy, reduced self-responsibility and subsequent demotivation. Enablers are convinced that, if an equivalent investment was made to develop the capability of the majority to cope with and adapt to change, the result would be a considerable improvement in morale and motivation.

Such a change in focus would encourage the majority to be responsible for their actions, aware of their environment and committed to make a positive contribution to improve their organization, community and society. The aim of the enabler is therefore to encourage individuals to perceive change as depicted by the developmental cycle model (Figure 10.4).

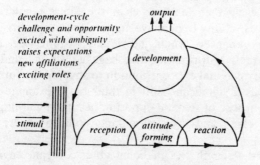

Figure 10.4   Developmental cycle

The factor which differentiates whether individuals are on a defensive developmental cycle is the attitudes they hold. Individuals on a developmental cycle approach change with a positive and constructive set of attitudes and perceive it as offering challenge and opportunities. They feel good and are excited by, and anticipative of, the potential positive outcomes. They generate the energy and develop visions which are translated into action. The enabler's task is to create environments within which an increasing number of people operate on a developmental cycle.

Investment in the majority

Investing in the majority would be a positive strategy designed to shape developmental cycle environments. Effort would be made to build self-esteem and provide recognition for the fine work being done and the value of its contribution to society. The aim would be to provide a counter balance to the negative forces by showing faith in the positive power and potential of the majority. Recognizing that every individual has the choice of being on a growth spiral rather than being sucked into a defensive cycle stimulates enablers to find ways to achieve the former. The two models have been combined below to illustrate the dynamic nature of the change process and where the point of choice is made (Figure 10.5).

Whereas we identified that individuals in a defensive cycle tend to clog their perceptual filters with negative factors, in the developmental cycle they learn to clear the filters regularly and so improve their ability to perceive and understand reality. Enabling change is enhanced when individuals acquire the ability to discharge their historical/negative baggage, let go, and begin to believe they can make a contribution to shaping the future. What is needed is a significant shift in thinking to examine problems with the purpose of seeking opportunities; then learning to apply solution-seeking and decision-making skills to ensure they are realized.

Enablers' strength lies in being able to create environments which enable an increasing number of individuals to make the transition from a defensive to developmental cycle. When achieved it releases the potential and power to transform lives, organizations and society. We see the enabling leader's role as

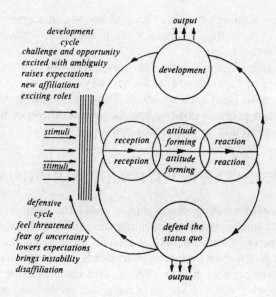

Figure 10.5 Combined defence and development cycles

one of facilitating the transition to a new state which enables individuals to transform society for the benefit of all.

Positive attitudes

Awareness of the change process allows individuals the opportunity to develop attitudes which enable them to make the best possible use of each changing situation. When enablers refer to developing positive attitudes it involves looking at each situation and defining the issues which change may raise, then addressing the issues with the purpose of recognizing how they can act to achieve results which enhance the situation and resolve the issues positively.

Many people are receptive to the analogy that developing themselves is like climbing a mountain. When they feel they have reached the summit, they look out over the horizon and see another peak just ahead. This may mean descending into a valley before they can climb towards the next peak of achievement. They accept that although they may have to invest considerable energy into the next climb, they have a vision and clarity about where they are trying to go.

Enabling leaders understand the ups and downs of life and have an attitude of looking forward to find ways of achieving the best possible result from each situation. They will be aware that each solution can produce positive and beneficial outcomes for those involved as well as to the wider population.

CHANGE STARTS WITH THE INDIVIDUAL

The thrust of enabling leadership is about the need to increase our ability and motivation to acquire the skills which enable us to cope effectively with change. We have approached the process with the philosophy that each of us needs to change first before we can ever expect others to change. This challenges the thinking of many who still believe they have the power and ability to change others in a way which meets their perception of what needs to be done.

The enabling change approach works on the principle of involving individuals in the process by providing them with the opportunity to explore each event which directly affects them. Assistance would initially be provided to enable them understand the implications of change and how these might affect them. Opportunities would also be provided for individuals to acquire and develop skills to analyse, understand and cope with change.

Help would come in the form of a framework to enable individuals to obtain a clear understanding of what the change involves as a step towards finding appropriate solutions. The following process, used by enablers, is a useful framework to help individuals understand what is involved:

- explore the change to discover the triggers involved
- assess the reasons and identify the need for change
- identify benefits which can be derived from change
- explore the risks involved to understand how they can be removed or reduced
- find ways to involve individuals in the change process, and keep them informed on what may happen at any point

- take time to explain perceived difficulties as this can avoid an overoptimistic view of the change process and bring realism into play
- set observable/measurable standards to enable all those involved to focus their energies in the desired direction and help the bystanders know how well it is progressing
- if things go wrong, keep everyone informed to prevent the 'grapevine' having a field day.

As individuals progress through the solution-seeking process enablers encourage them to be open and creative in their search for ideas. They also seek out and work with individuals who are either the formal or informal leaders of opinion in the situation. The aim is to involve them in the process and obtain their support in hastening solutions to a satisfactory conclusion.

Making decisions and receiving feedback

The enabling process is designed to create an environment which allows individuals the freedom to reach a point at which they feel able to make decisions about how they wish to respond to change. Within this constructive environment every effort is made to encourage them to accept full responsibility for their response to change. They also learn to be aware of how their actions impact on others and the effect this might have on the outcomes. Awareness of the interdependent nature of actions taken to achieve results are developed to enable individuals to understand how to respond to change responsibly.

To aid the process, enablers find opportunities to provide feedback on performance as a means of offering encouragement and praise for achievement. This also helps create a supportive climate which sets a tone of endeavour and commitment to the task. When progress is satisfactory it makes sense to provide feedback to act as positive reinforcement for the value of the contributions being made.

Individuals are able to cope with situations in an enabling manner when they understand what is happening and feel able to manage the change process. Feedback is an essential part of the process as it provides information on the state of play. How it is communicated plays an important part in creating an enabling environment of achievement in which individuals feel able to make an appropriate contribution. Discovering where, when and how to make their contribution is an essential stage in the process. This requires careful, aware and sensitive exploration of each change situation to identify the most effective points of intervention.

POINTS OF INTERVENTION

We have established that an enabling leader's response to change involves scanning the horizon to detect strategic signposts which flag current and future directions. As they undertake the scanning process this enables them to identify:

- indicators
- opportunities
- solutions.

Indicators

As we develop awareness we begin to notice indicators which help us understand the effects of change. At the present time there are many professional people involved in studying the past to try to discover indicators which enable them to predict the future. The rapid rate of change means that we can depend less on this method to predict the future as a number of factors increasingly bear little relationship to current events. Studying these involves making an extremely complex matrix which, even with the power of computers, is difficult to unravel in order to identify the effect any one factor might have on the total picture.

Another method of exploring strategic directions is for individuals to learn to project their minds into the future (see Chapter 2). They choose a particular date in the future and then apply their creative and imaginative powers to construct scenarios of what they perceive could exist. Current signposts would act as indicators with perceived results being explored using a creative thinking process. The various scenarios are assessed resulting in a composite picture which best represents the desired future.

A useful refinement to the analysis process involved a reverse projection which enables a return to the present. Gaps can be identified in the organization's resources and direction which could accelerate or restrain progress towards its vision of the future.

Strategic directions

If people get in the habit of living in the present with positive attitudes about the future, they are more able to determine strategic directions. This can enable the effects of change to be harnessed for the benefit of society. For example, a great deal of energy and concern is being put into defending jobs. Considerable emotional and factual reasons are provided to justify the action taken to preserve these jobs. Yet the outcome of this energy appears to reduce the number of jobs rather than retaining or even increasing job opportunities.

The reasons are fairly straightforward when you examine the results of change in the world market over the past decade. Instead of channelling energy into preserving jobs using traditional, labour-intensive methods more relevant to the 1950s, we need to examine new options and adopt strategies which recognize that increased productivity may involve working in different ways, using different methods and in some instances with fewer people to create the products/services which are saleable. Efforts extended in these directions would have a greater chance of retaining jobs and providing a basis for potential growth resulting in new job opportunities.

I have no doubt that looking for the indicators which flag what is happening on the macro-scale will provide clear signposts on what should be done to take advantage, and achieve benefits, at the micro-level. This will involve developing a habit of scanning environments to detect those trends and indicators. It also involves us in discarding the historical baggage which is no longer relevant, and reduces our ability to seek solutions appropriate to the age we live in.

Seeking opportunities

Believing that benefits can be realized from situations created by change means that enablers actively look for opportunities rather than the problems associated with change. They want to examine the situation to identify what actually exists and isolate the factors associated with the change situation. There may be factors which appear to be inevitable and which nothing can be done to change. However on further examination and looking at it from different viewpoints, they are able to find possibilities and opportunities.

Believing that opportunities do exist enables them to find them even in the most difficult and seemingly hopeless situations. There is a lot of talk about the decline of the 'sunset' industries in developed countries. Those who study its effects recognize that it is largely due to a wide range of factors which include:

- transfer of labour-intensive industries to developing countries as part of an international development strategy to 'industrialize' them
- increase in labour costs which price traditional products out of the market
- innovation which encourages developed countries to become more technological and service-oriented
- rising aspirations of individuals in developed countries to improve their standard of living
- dramatic fluctuations in the marketplace caused by political and economic decisions
- steady decline in world markets due to successive economic recessions and slower recoveries.

Many analysts accept the inevitability of the decline of 'sunset' and growth of 'sunrise' industries. Yet the inevitable may be questioned as technological innovation changes the economic factors. The technological revolution has produced artificially intelligent machines and processes which means that developed countries can once again regain a cost advantage with traditional products associated with 'sunset' industries.

We may now experience a revival of fortunes through the regrowth of traditional industries in developed countries by using frontier technology to recapture their competitive advantage once more. The lesson to learn from the above is the value of developing an effective strategic thinking process and practice which looks beyond the frontiers of current thinking. Stretching our thinking outside the 'dots' is a valuable analogy for individuals to adopt as they search for solutions to the change scenarios being developed.

Solution-seeking

Developing a focus on opportunities gives the enabler a wider range of options to achieve positive results from each change. As enablers explore the issue and identify the factors involved, they produce a map which suggests potential strategic directions. The map enables the issue to be viewed from a number of different perspectives, using positive thinking to identify potential solutions.

Enablers understand that the key to finding solutions relates to the attitudes individuals adopt about change. Recognizing that change is inevitable, and will affect everyone in different ways, provides a stimulus to manage its effects and achieve positive results. Awareness of change, and its effects, provides individuals with an increasing understanding of what can be done to achieve the best possible results from situations brought about by change. They replace the fear of change with expectancy and excitement in seeking solutions to situations they encounter.

Points of intervention

Developing an organizational culture which encourages individuals within the organization to be positive and responsive to change requires an understanding of the change process. We discussed earlier the need for individuals to 'buy into' organizational values as a means of enabling them to internalize and express the values through congruent behaviour. Given that the culture is designed to enable its organizational members to view change as a challenge and opportunity, it will thus enhance its ability to respond in the most positive way.

There are generally two modes of action to manage change

situations. One involves waiting until change occurs and then reacting by developing strategies and tactics to achieve the best possible outcomes from the situation. The other involves thinking about a range of possible future scenarios which change may bring and developing contingency plans to meet the challenge. This latter process is termed 'being proactive' and involves mapping possible courses of action designed to anticipate rather than react to change. When an organization operates in a proactive mode, it usually copes more effectively through a process of planned interventions within its organization, market and community.

Awareness of the need to intervene

As an organization develops its ability to paint scenarios of the future, it will identify the adverse and positive consequences of certain actions it may take. Understanding the consequences of each action taken or proposed can clarify when the organization should change its policy, practice, methods, personnel, etc. We call the points of change 'intervention points' and encourage organizations to identify when and where to intervene to achieve effective results from perceived and actual areas of change.

As individuals learn and practise visioning, analysis of the scenarios should enable them to identify where they need to intervene in the organization. This enhances their ability to respond positively to perceived threats/opportunities created by change. As they learn from feedback the successes and failures of interventions, they increase awareness of where, when and how interventions should take place. The process also develops clarity about why the intervention is required and the expected outcomes.

Purpose of intervention

Recognizing that interventions are designed to bring about a variety of outcomes, it is vital that the specific purpose of an intervention be understood. This should be spelled out in clear terms. As individuals identify intervention points, they will also need to establish objectives/outcomes for the intervention.

Irrespective of the level in an organization at which the intervention takes place,it will involve people. The benefits and effects need to be communicated to help individuals understand how the process will meet their needs. The more specifically the intervention describes the part individuals will play in the process, the more likely they will add value and help with the intervention. The enabling leader will work within organizations to assist individuals understand the importance of being aware of how change interventions relate to, and may affect, their jobs.

ENABLING CHANGE

All enablers will develop a mission statement which expresses their attitude and motivation to enabling change. The mission is clearly focused on achieving positive results from the process of managing change. It recognizes that opportunities are available, provides incentives to search for those opportunities, and seeks solutions which fit the strategic directions identified. As the strategy takes shape, it will involve enablers in a process of examining their values and beliefs and modifying them to take account of any new focus and direction.

The enabler recognizes that standing still in this rapidly changing world implies that individuals regress. Being open and learning to look forward helps enablers build awareness of what can be done to obtain satisfactory results. As they have a results orientation, solutions will be identified and examined to envision what the potential outputs could be.

Working at translating the vision into reality will be done within a framework of considering other options on an ongoing basis. This is an exciting part of the enabler's ability to manage change in that their antennae are constantly looking for options which could produce better results. As their ability to manage change improves, the rate of achieving positive results increases and can be seen as an example in practice of what can be done.

Helping others cope with change

Working with individuals to help them examine their attitudes is an important step in helping them learn to cope with change. The aim is to help them replace negative feelings with an attitude of positive expectancy. This is the process used to assist them face and learn to understand all the forces of change. Enabling is carried out within the philosophy expressed earlier and using enabling skills to equip individuals to manage change in their own way. Individuals focus on what 'can', rather than what 'cannot', be done. It is about enabling an individual to be confident about meeting the challenge of change, and understanding that the solutions developed are unique to them. As confidence builds it can reinforce the value of learning to develop a self-managed change process.

We support the developing practice in many organizations of actively involving individuals in the solution-seeking and decision-making process. It enables them to understand the changes taking place and provides opportunities for them to adapt. Most individuals have the potential to be creative in seeking solutions. However, this potential talent may not be fully realized if they do not operate in an environment which encourages them to participate in the process of managing change.

We saw earlier how the change process starts with the individual and how becoming an enabling leader involves varying degrees of change as individuals modify their thinking, behaviour and actions. As enablers progress through a personal change process, they learn to perceive the benefits an awareness of its effects provides. This awareness is of importance when they are enabling others to cope with change. It can help the enabling leader to empathize with each individual in a congruent manner.

As an increasing number of individuals become enabling leaders they form positive groups for change and develop centres of enabling. Each group may eventually connect to create a world-wide network of enablers committed to enabling change in a senstive and effective manner. This ever-increasing number will influence society towards creating environments which encourage people to be in a developmental cycle.

Release of positive energy and creativity will promote the generation of solutions to many of the problems faced by individuals, organizations and nations all over the world. Problems will be confronted with determination, willingness and a curiosity to discover the opportunities on offer. Solutions will be found which provide creative ways for individuals to be involved in enabling positive change to occur.

Glossary

Achievement
 the result of an individual contributing from his/her ASK tool kit to achieve an agreed goal.

Achievement Review
 an interactive and dynamic process used to provide objective feedback on individual's performance against agreed and shared goals.

Active Listening
 involves demonstrating to speakers by the use of appropriate feedback that they are being heard.

Add Value
 an individual's, or team's, contribution to agreed goals that represents an improvement on what existed before.

Agenda
 the issues individuals wish to have considered when involved in a particular transaction which affects them.

ASK
 an acronym for the attitudes, skills and knowledge that learning attempts to enhance.

Awareness
 the ability to 'read' a situation to determine what is happening and assess the appropriate action to take.

Behaviour
 the written, oral and non-oral actions of individuals as they interact with others.

Buy-in

the positive action taken by individuals to accept a decision reached after a process which has involved them in arriving at the decision. When an individual 'buys-in' there is no further question of the individual's commitment to the decision and subsequent action.

Climate
a set of conditions in an organization which influences individuals to act and behave in a particular manner.

Coach
the involvement of an experienced individual in assisting another individual(s) in a planned and enabling manner to acquire agreed ASK.

Competitive Advantage
the factors which make one organization more effective and successful than others.

Consensus
a process which involves individuals in exploring issues in an open and constructive manner designed to enable all to 'buy-in' to any decisions made.

Contribution
an individual's willingness to apply his/her ASK toolkit in adding value to meet the needs of an agreed common purpose.

Culture
a set of values which are shared and used by individuals within an organization, and understood by those outside the organization.

Effective
able to accomplish an activity successfully within the agreed plan.

Efficient
able to perform to high standards, established by the individual or group, which may or may not add value to the organization's outputs.

Empathy
understanding and recognizing the feelings of other individuals, and projecting that understanding through appropriate feedback.

Enable

to empower individuals to act in a manner which adds value to a transaction .

Enabler

an individual who empowers others, through practising enabling leadership, to act in a positive manner and adds value to whatever is being done for the common good.

Enabling Culture

a set of shared values designed to foster growth and development of the individual within a caring and sharing environment thus enabling effective contributions to be made.

Enabling Environment

a set of conditions (see environment) in an organization which motivates individuals to be actively involved in achieving desired outputs, because they are actively involved in shaping the culture and its goals.

Enabling Leadership

an environment which energizes every individual to achieve the highest level of performance to fulfil agreed goals.

Enabling Organization

one which has a clearly stated mission and shared values which define its culture, values people and produces an environment of achievement.

Environment

the conditions and influences which affect the contribution an individual will make. These include:

– physical location and condition
– culture as expressed by the shared values
– systems and procedures
– each individual's frame of reference
– external environmental influences.

Environmental Scanning

the searching of both internal and external environments to detect trends which may have some effect on an individual or an organization in maintaining its competitive advantage.

Envision

to see as a vision, to visualize, to envisage a mental view of a desired state in the future.

Frame of Reference

the values, prejudice, bias, expectations and other elements which form the 'eyes' through which individuals view the world in general and a situation in particular.

Gems

refers to the 'ah ha's' which occur and which we recommend should be captured for future reference. (The term 'gem' comes from India and is a trade name for a paper clip which is used to attach ideas together.)

Geodesic Dome

a light strong dome made by combining a grid of triangular or other straight line elements with a section of a sphere. Normally associated with the work of Buckminster Fuller.

Goal

an observable and measurable activity which has a specific end result.

Groundrules

a set of rules which provide a framework to enable two or more individuals to transact in a positive manner designed to achieve desired outputs.

Historical Baggage

the part of an individual's experience which contaminates thinking about, and acting in, the present and future.

Knowing/Doing Syndrome

the difference between understanding a concept and being able to translate it into behaviour, perceived by others as congruent.

Learning

a process which enables individuals to acquire additional ASK.

Mind Set

the particular set of values and beliefs which individuals use to form attitudes to an issue, or individual, and which may eventually be translated into the behaviours they display.

Mission

the vision individuals have of the organization's future expressed in a form which provides direction and guidance to all those involved. Applies equally to an individual.

Motivation

a complex set of values which enables individuals to perceive a benefit (or avoid pain) which activates them to make an effective contribution.

Objective
> similar to goal except that it tends to be used to describe outputs with a longer timeframe.

Openness
> a state of behaviour used by individuals which stimulates others to believe that their transactions will be carried out in a climate of trust and sharing.

Outcomes/Outputs
> the observable/measurable result of each individual's contribution to achievement of agreed goals.

Participative Management
> a process used to involve all individuals engaged in an organization in decision-making on issues which affect them. This means achieving results 'with' individuals rather than 'through' them.

Polygon
> a plain figure bounded by more than four straight lines.

Polysphere
> the interaction of all the polygons which form our vision of the future. It has a spherical shape, yet is not contained by a circle.

Proactive
> differs from reactive in that individuals develop an ability to think ahead of issues and to develop plans to meet well thought out contingencies associated with each action.

Process
> a state of being in progress involving a series of actions with people to achieve a desired outcome.

Professional
> the quality of an individual's contribution as displayed through the application of his/her ASK portfolio to the achievement of agreed goals.

Revisit
> re-examine a previous issue in the awareness that factors will most likely have changed. It means undertaking the examination as if it were for the first time.

Scenario
> picture of a desired state produced from the perceptions gleaned during environmental scanning and comprising a variety of elements including indicators, trends and direc-

tions, which represent an internally consistent view of what
the future may look like.

Self-Awareness
an ability to interpret interpersonal transaction and associated
environments in a way which enables individuals to act in a
positive manner and achieve effective outcomes.

Self-Leadership
a state of individual competence which enables individuals to
assume leadership roles when making their contribution.

Strategic Direction
interpretation of strategic indicators and trends to determine
a strategy which points in a specific direction which if taken
could enable the organization to maintain its competitive
advantage.

Strategy
the development of a plan which describes what an organization aims to achieve from an agreed direction through the
deployment of specific resources and tactics.

Transaction
interpersonal interaction between two or more individuals
who meet for some purpose.

Value
the clusters of beliefs held by an individual which are formed
during his/her lifespan.

Visionary
individual who perceives vivid concepts or sees mental
pictures of a future event and expresses imaginative plans
which he/she has developed in anticipation of being involved
in its creation.

Win/Win
the outcome of a transaction which results in all parties feeling
that they have gained benefits, whilst taking account of the
prevailing circumstances.